BETTER MINDS

ELKE GERAERTS

BETTER MINDS

How Insourcing Strengthens Resilience
and Empowers Your Brain

 LANNOO

*To all those who have encouraged, challenged
and strengthened my mental resilience*

Contents

· ·

INTRODUCTION
OUTSOURCING IS OUT, INSOURCING IS IN

PART I
A WAY THROUGH THE BRAIN CRISIS

PART II
PROFITING FROM RESILIENCE

PART III
FOUR WAYS TO ARRIVE
AT A BETTER BRAIN STRATEGY

CONCLUSION
GROWING THROUGH CRISIS

OUTSOURCING IS OUT, INSOURCING IS IN

Something is wrong. We all feel it, it's just taken us a long time to put our finger on it. Something is wrong, though on paper we're doing better than ever. Our entire lives are optimized. Our companies are full of specialists whose professionalism is supplemented by courses and additional training. In our social lives we leave almost nothing to chance and in our personal lives we in the West have no reason to complain. We are healthier, live longer and seem freer than ever before. And yet we still feel that something is wrong.

THE BRAIN CRISIS

For years, we've seen the number of psychological problems increasing in both adults and children. At first we thought the increase could be attributed to improved detection. The more you look, and the better you know what you're looking for, the more you find. Now we know better. Suicides, addictions, attention, anxiety and eating disorders, depression and neuroses do in fact occur more frequently today than they did several decades ago. Selling antidepressants has become one of the most profitable industries of the 21st century. The World Health Organization (WHO) estimates that by 2020, depression will be the most common disease in Western countries — even more than heart failure. And on top of that there's burnout.

Burnout is not a new disease, but in recent years it has experienced an increase of epidemic proportions. The WHO is on the point of declaring the condition a pandemic, given its dramatic growth over the past decade. Prevalence studies based on the Maslach Burnout Inventory, the standard test for burnout since 1981, paint an alarming picture of the international spread of the condition. In the United States and the United Kingdom, where burnout levels run to over 30 percent, the situation is dramatic. Even more worrying is the fact that these figures seem to be only the tip of the iceberg. Of the employees who do not (yet) have burnout, around half experience stress and one in four experience physical and psychological symptoms that interfere with their productivity.

These are staggering figures that, if we look closely, all point in the same direction: our brain. Stress, burnout, mental problems: they are usually to be found, quite literally, in our heads. The most important organ in our body, the greatest asset a person has at their disposal, is suffering under the speed and pressure of modern times. I would even go so far as to say that our brains show signs of intense neglect. With all the consequences this entails.

THE DANGERS OF OUTSOURCING

With our big brains, we have created a new world for ourselves, but the longer it continues, the more it is undermining our brains. The term used to describe this is VUCA: the Volatile, Uncertain, Complex and Ambiguous society that comes with globalization. A society we have created, but not chosen. In the VUCA world, change follows change in rapid succession, certainties are rare, all problems are too complex to grasp, and the risk of misunderstanding is extremely high. In themselves, these challenges might not be much more difficult than the challenges of a century ago, but they are certainly different. It's just that our heads can't keep up. Or, not at the speed we want them to. And so we go looking for easy solutions. Companies try to outsource as much as possible by allocating tasks that used to be handled by "brain-workers" (like the secretaries of yesteryear) to digital systems and devices. Today, everyone can manage his or her own agenda, correspondence, documents and job scheduling and now that it's all so easy, we also do it en masse. The smartphone has become an indispensable part of our daily lives. It's certainly convenient, but whether it really takes a load off our brain is another question. Recent research suggests that digitization is an important new challenge for our brain.

And so we continue spinning around in the same vicious circle. To give our brain some relief, we create new tools that overstimulate it to such a degree that we have to devise new tools to relieve it again. We're focused on stop-gap measures, without getting any closer to the heart of the matter. To put it in financial terms: we're spending a lot of money but there's not enough fresh capital coming in. We aren't investing, we're making losses. But it doesn't have to be this way. Instead of outsourcing, we could be "insourcing." Instead of fighting the symptoms, we could be overcoming this brain crisis by aiming straight for the goal. We need to step out of this vicious circle and give our brains a much-needed capital injection. Because we can, and because we must.

It sounds like a massive cliché, but every cloud has a silver lining. Because the brain crisis is claiming more and more victims, emergency signals are, fortunately, starting to flash. Brave people are sounding the alarm, making burnout and other stress-related problems easier to discuss. The media pay a lot of attention to the subject, and even policy now takes burnout prevention into account. I also see more and more companies, institutions, organizations and individuals begin to invest in their own mental resilience and that of their coworkers. But such investment is not obvious. Most leaders have a great deal of expertise when it comes to dealing with financial capital, but their most important means of production – the brains of their employees – remains a mystery.

Thanks to recent scientific research, we know more about what makes people resilient and how we can empower our brain. Too often this knowledge is purely theoretical; it's time to put it into practice.

As a scientist, I have conducted research into psychological problems in several countries. This inspired me to look at the other side of the coin – namely, how we can turn a psychological disadvantage into an advantage.

Our consultancy firm Better Minds at Work offers know-how and customized programs for reinforcing mental resilience in companies and organizations. With this book, I want to take an important step forwards by making this knowledge available to everyone. I'm convinced that the current brain crisis with all its challenges is also an enormous opportunity for growth. Let's turn the tide before it's too late. The time has come to invest in our minds, both on an individual level and at the level of organizations and companies.

GROWING THROUGH CRISIS

I'm certainly not alone in demanding that our brains get a major capital injection. Many companies realize that they have to invest in the well-being of their employees. I'm also very glad there are moves to make burnout a legally recognized phenomenon. These are important initial steps towards a more positive brain strategy that enable us to reduce burnout and other stress-related problems considerably, and also ensure we emerge from the crisis stronger than ever. By investing in our minds, we will not only break the downward spiral and prevent burnout, we will also become more creative, more productive and happier. To put it in financial terms again: we will not only recuperate our losses and break even, we will also turn a profit.

I realize this might sound utopian, but recent developments in brain studies have given reasons for optimism. Research into the brain in the last few decades has increased exponentially. Until the 1950s, scientists considered our brains to be the private domain of philosophers, but since then research in psychology and biology has developed at lightning speed. "The decade of the brain," the 1990s, has yielded numerous surprising new insights. Thanks to MRI (magnetic resonance imaging) scans, we can make impressively detailed photos in which the structure of our brain is clearly visible, and with fMRI scans (functional MRI, in which brain activity is also viewed), we can see how thoughts and feelings wander around in our heads, and observe and analyze their movements. My own discipline, psychology, has in the last 20 years managed to pry itself loose from being a "soft branch" of science. We now know more than ever about the functioning of our minds, emotions, behavior, love, despair and all other aspects of life. Moreover, since the 1990s, psychology and neuroscience aren't restricted to finding solutions for sick people; they actively search for ways to make life better and more enjoyable for everyone. The recipes for success, engagement and happiness are increasingly up for grabs.

Today we are more than ever able to define what makes our mind strong and resilient: how self-control and perseverance can determine our whole lives, how we can use our consciousness both consciously and unconsciously, why focus is so difficult to maintain, and how optimism not only makes us happier, but also more successful.

Not only do we know the building blocks better, thanks to brain research we also know what we can do with them and how we can train them. Self-control, consciousness, focus and optimism are not just innate characteristics, but skills we can develop and deploy in order to better our minds. Together they make up our resilience, the mental variant of flexibility and muscular strength. In keynote talks I often compare the two literally. I ask the audience whether they can imagine being able to train their brains the way you can train your muscles in the gym. And then you see people nodding: yes, that would be really nice. Well, it's possible: you can strengthen your brain and in this way protect yourself against burnout and stress. In this book, I want to share this knowledge with you.

I am convinced we have sufficient knowledge to overcome the brain crisis, to become mentally stronger and more resilient than ever before, and – not least – to give the next generation sufficient startup capital to meet the challenges of the future with confidence.

The possibility exists, as I hope to make clear in this book. But the need to do it also exists. The figures are already alarming and if we don't want to lose our heads in the 21st century, then we have to start putting the knowledge we've built up about the brain to good use. We already face new challenges: work processes are changing, technology is surpassing our congnitive ability, the pace of life is increasing and social structures are being undermined. In this world, self-knowledge is much more than "the beginning of wisdom," but a prerequisite for survival. Those who don't take their own neurological basis seriously will discover the consequences sooner or later. And those consequences are increasingly appearing sooner rather than later.

If we don't urgently move forward with this knowledge, I predict that stress-related problems will increase. Psychology can play an important role here as a brake on this negative spiral, but also – and particularly – as a protection against new problems. With each new invention lurks a new danger. Resiliently anticipating these challenges is not as optional as it seems.

Investing in our minds is not only the most effective tool against stress and burnout, it is also the way to emerge from the crisis stronger and to prepare ourselves for the 21st century. Easier said than done? Perhaps. But do we really have a choice? I firmly believe that we owe this investment to ourselves, our brains and our children. Let's not wait until our society completely collapses because we've neglected our brains; let's choose resolutely in favor of a brain boost.

PART I

A WAY THROUGH THE BRAIN CRISIS

Portrait of a burnout

. . . .

Not a month goes by when we don't hear about burnout in the news. Each time with harder facts and figures, more confrontational analyses. Still, the column that Laurent Winnock, director of communication and corporate responsibility at insurer AXA Belgium, wrote about his experience with burnout is one of the most striking I've ever read. Because his column still echoes in my mind, I'd like to share it with you.

LAURENT'S STORY

Exactly one year ago, I dropped out with a case of burnout. I still see myself sitting in the car, rocked by crying fits because I was "burned out," until the light literally went out at the doctor's office. However bad that period may have been, I still think of it as my greatest opportunity. Not everyone is lucky enough to be able to make a new start at the age of 35 after suffering from depression.

How did it get to this point? Let me call it a combination of structural professional excess and an emotional violation of important professional values, sanctioned by me. In addition, I neglected my body and mind for years in a continuous cycle of neglect and adrenaline-fueled excess.

In retrospect, it's easy to ask why I didn't realize that I couldn't sleep, suffered from back pain and never managed to shake that constant cough. That I abandoned friends and hobbies. That my long days at work, where I was hyper-irritable with those around me, weren't normal. I know that now, and also that no one tried to stop me.

The first days of burnout are hell. All those repressed physical ailments come to the surface and you're exhausted after walking half a block. But it's the mental emptiness that is most painful of all. It was only after those first few weeks that my brain became active again, but I still wasn't healed. No, in my eyes, the external world was the culprit: it was all the fault of somebody else. In my case, that was partly true, but it was only when I realized that the cause of my burnout was a shared responsibility could I begin my mental healing process.

I was guided the whole time by my wonderful physician and fantastic therapist. I still see the latter every month to talk about how I'm progressing and how I approach things differently. I will continue to do so, and I recommend it to everyone. In addition, I received so much loving care from my immediate environment, and I could count on a lot of understanding and support from my professional environment and my CEO.

But this is only the starting point. The most difficult part is maintaining the daily discipline needed to organize my work better and in ways that are more healthy, to enjoy my work and especially to enjoy what happens outside of work. Initiating a process of change had its ups and downs, but gradually it began to work. I ditched the agenda parasites; now I'm very selective about meetings and only attend those where my presence brings added value. I take time to take distance, to reflect and to be inspired. I set aside time to be with my teams and just hang out. During intense work periods I plan energizing projects. I put work away to spend time with my loved ones and take regular walks during periods when there's not much on the *calendar. "What a life of luxury," I hear you thinking. I prefer to call it a sustainable life. Because make no mistake, I still have to perform for my company and achieve daily objectives with essential cost savings. And since I've started working differently, I do that more successfully than before.*

Why am I saying this now? Because I had to discover the hard way that we all perform like top athletes every day, but without the necessary preparation. A top athlete takes into account the balance between mental and physical rest and performance, says no to things that don't fit in his or her program, and talks to the trainer if the latter isn't showing the way to top performance. In the sports world, this is quite normal.

How does the business world differ? In many organizations, the mental well-being of human capital still doesn't get the attention it deserves. But we as individuals are often not aware of what a healthy work ethic involves.

How often have I heard colleagues and bosses say that they're too busy, have lost control of their agenda, and are under so much pressure... but that they can't say no? What really gets to me are the testimonies of courageous fellow human beings who openly admit that they suffer constant abdominal or back pain because of stress, but don't know how to deal with it differently. It all sounds so familiar. Unfortunately, many, many more don't dare speak up for fear of being viewed as weak in an organizational culture that is not open to the idea. They're the ones who really need help.

Ten percent of the workforce is at home with burnout; five percent are in the critical zone. I've been lucky enough to have an employer that gave me lots of support and has been working on a structural approach to wellness. I hope my testimony

motivates many others to take action. And for those who cling
stubbornly to old ways: a sick employee costs more than a
healthy one. And now for a bit of recovery.

SHARED RESPONSIBILITY

For me, what makes Winnock's column so powerful is that he writes without blame. Ever since burnout was recognized as an occupational illness, employers have often felt like scapegoats, even though this is not always true. In some cases the blame is formulated explicitly. In France, the former CEO of France Telecom was summoned to court after more than 30 employees attempted to commit suicide in one year. He was accused of promoting a corporate culture that drove employees over the edge. In Japan, too, employers run serious risks if their employees commit suicide, particularly if the latter regularly did overtime in the months leading up to their death. In that case, the death falls under the category "karoshi," or "death by burnout," in which both the government and the company executives have to pay damages to the family. In China, there is also a term for "death by burnout" (*guolaosi*), and companies are considered responsible for the well-being of their personnel.

Without denying that executives have a responsibility and that they can influence corporate culture positively or negatively, I think we cannot get around the fact that the burnout epidemic comes from a broader context that companies do not always comprehend. Moreover, the burnout epidemic is not exclusively limited to employees. Several studies show that freelance entrepreneurs run an even greater risk of burnout than people with paid employment. Business leaders form another important risk group. When we look at burnout among senior management, recent research from the Harvard Business School shows that 96 percent of senior managers feel "a little burned out." One in three describes the feeling as "extremely burned out."

In corporate life, a director might be the loneliest person there is. He or she is always expected to be alert and never to have a bad day. The same characteristics that drive executives to the top, such as their stamina, help hide the fact that something is wrong – even from themselves. People can continue on autopilot for a long time, but the crash will eventually occur, even for executives. When it does, the company often suffers from a domino effect. The workload falls on the shoulders of others, they have more work on their plates and are in turn more susceptible to burnout. And so on. In this way, a company can find itself in a dangerous vicious circle.

BURNED-OUT VOLUNTEERS

The risks for those with burnout are considerable. Among others, Wilmar Schaufeli, a world authority on burnout research at the University of Utrecht, has shown that people with burnout run a greater risk of developing chronic fatigue, alcoholism, sleep disorders, neck pain and other physical health problems. In a study spread out over ten years, Finnish professor Kirsi Ahola showed that burnout was linked to a 35-percent higher chance of death among employees who were younger than 45 when the study began.

Whenever I disclose these figures, people are surprised and disbelieving. "If burnout is such a big problem, why are we only hearing about it now?" I've heard that a lot. But it's not quite correct. The term "burnout" might sound new, but we've actually been confronted with the problem for years. Only, it was called "stress" until very recently. Stress in and of itself is not necessarily a problem; a limited amount of stress can have a positive effect. For example, a small peak in stress just before I give a lecture ensures that I'm more alert, that I reach a certain level of focus, and that I can concentrate fully on my lecture and interaction with the public. Researcher Kelly McGonigal of Stanford University has even proposed that stress is your friend as long as you learn how to handle it well and use it in order to perform. Stress becomes a problem, however, when the burden (the amount of stress or seriousness of the stressful situation) is greater than our capacity to bear it (the resources we have for dealing with the situation). Chronic stress can undermine a person and eventually lead to burnout. For the psychologists who warned us for so many years that stress levels in society were too high, the burnout crisis certainly comes as no surprise.

Likewise, the term "burnout" is not so new. The concept was launched around 40 years ago by the psychologist Herbert Freudenberger, who advised volunteers in New York in the 1970s. Freudenberger noticed that these people, who were at first full of enthusiasm and dedication to their work, began to show serious symptoms of emotional exhaustion and loss of motivation after a few months. One of his respondents described feeling "burned out." All mental and physical energy was gone, all desire to continue was lost, all job satisfaction extinguished.

Around the same time, on the other side of the United States, in California, similar symptoms were discovered among social workers. Psychologists Christina Maslach and Susan Jackson first described "burnout" as "emotional exhaustion, depersonalization, and the disappearance of the feeling of accomplishment." Their description of burnout as a combination of these three phenomena is now generally accepted.

Thanks to the pioneering work of these psychologists, the phenomenon of burnout is known to researchers around the world and has been studied extensively. Since then, many thousands have been diagnosed with the condition, but there has been an increase in recent years. Until around a decade ago, burnout was mainly known as a typical illness among welfare workers, but it has now penetrated all levels of society. As a consequence, "burnout" has also become a buzzword. Many people use it colloquially when they experience periods of stress. Recently someone said to me: "Last week I had a little burnout because that deadline was just too stressful." The danger is that burnout will no longer be taken seriously. I once heard an employee sigh: "Nowadays everyone has burnout when they have too much going on in their private life." The reality, of course, is somewhere in the middle: people all too readily proclaim "I have burnout!" – but this does not mean that real burnout is less problematic.

TECHNOLOGY AND ROLE STRESS

Burnout may have first turned up officially among volunteers in the 1970s, but today it is no longer limited to the edges of the welfare sector. What is it about our labor market that has changed substantially? Why do thousands of people have the same symptoms as jaded social workers in the 1970s? What do our jobs have in common with those of volunteers? The answer, I believe, is both the amount of work we do, and the way we work.

One thing very particular to the job of volunteers and social workers is that it never ends. Great social commitment all too often comes at the cost of privacy and emotional rest. Your work occupies you long after the working day is over. And what is the most important change in our lives since the start of the 21st century? The technological revolution.

First there was the home computer, then the laptop, the mobile phone, and now the smartphone. We are connected with each other all the time and everywhere, and hence with our work as well. In the last century, you left your office and it took until the next morning before you could go back to work. Now you can work anywhere, all the time, and too many people have to do exactly that. For me it is clear that the burnout epidemic is largely driven by modern technology.

A second characteristic that today's employees share with yesterday's volunteers and social workers is what is known in psychology as "role stress." In the 20th century, most jobs were fairly narrow and clearly defined. Everyone had his or her own competence for which he or she was 100 percent responsible. Today, things are different: everything revolves around flexibility, omni-employability and multitasking. This makes it difficult for many people to define what they do: not only to others, but also to themselves. "What exactly do you do?" used to be a difficult question for social workers. Today it's a difficult question for almost everyone.

Uncertainty about job responsibilities is one of the most important predictors of burnout. Role stress deprives people of the feeling that they have control over their job. They feel like a pawn in the hands of their superiors. Because of role stress, people are no longer able to develop or improve themselves. They simply don't know how. Lack of clarity concerning their exact function also means that it is harder to evaluate employees. Even the feeling of satisfaction with the end product for which you were responsible falls away. Role stress contributes to the development of a "helper syndrome," in which people take on all tasks in order to get ahead. Role stress also makes people feel uncertain about their own value and ensures that they don't dare complain. Above all, role stress is hopeless. You're never finished, nothing ever really succeeds, and there is always another pile of tasks waiting for you.

I think many people will recognize themselves in the description above. In a certain sense, we in the 21st century have all become social workers. Because of the changed technological context, and also the changed requirements of the labor market.

PERSONALITY AS A PREDICTIVE FACTOR

Although the changing context means that more people than ever are suffering from burnout, burnout is never (really never) to blame on context alone. It is always twofold: context and personality. Just as some social workers and volunteers work their entire lives without ever burning out, some people have no problem sleeping with their smartphone, doing the most diverse tasks for years on end – and never ending up with burnout.

So what determines who will suffer from burnout and who won't? The risk depends in part on your profession. According to recent polls, nurses, dentists, teachers, bankers and small businesses run the greatest risk. But if we look at the individual personality traits of people with burnout, it is also possible to define clear risk groups. Introverts are more at risk than extroverts because they're less quick to turn to resources for help, such as asking for feedback from colleagues. People who lack self-confidence or are emotionally unstable are more at risk. A tendency towards depression doesn't have a one-to-one relationship with an increased risk of burnout (depression is an emotional disorder, while burnout is an energy disorder), but it can be a factor. Perfectionists and idealists also have to watch out. Perfectionists are never satisfied with their performance, and do not feel fulfilled. The work is never finished, so they can never enjoy the results. Idealists, on the other hand, strive for such elevated goals that they often cross the boundary into exhaustion without noticing.

THE IMPORTANCE OF MENTAL FLEXIBILITY

At first glance, the description of risk factors for burnout might seem demotivating. Most people probably recognize themselves in one or several categories. Moreover, many assume that traits like perfectionism or self-confidence are largely fixed. If you're a perfectionist and/or a nurse, are you doomed to suffer burnout sooner or later? Not at all. There are many people who, on paper at least, are greatly at risk but will never suffer burnout. One perfectionistic nurse is clearly not the same as another. But what makes one succumb to pressure while the other only comes out stronger?

The answer is resilience. Mental flexibility, the ability to deal with adversity, determines how susceptible we are to stress and thus how great our risk of burnout really is (in spite of contextual and personality elements). The good news is that resilience, like muscle strength, can be developed and trained. That's what I want to focus on in this book. But if we want to avoid burnout, we must focus on more than just our brain. We must also maintain our physical resilience. We know from research that those who eat a healthy diet and get enough exercise are better able to cope with stress. Energy-rich, whole foods can help to keep your mind sharp, and sports help you work off the tension accumulated through stress. Moreover, you can banish stressful thoughts while exercising, so that your mind becomes clear again. Sufficient sleep is also crucial in maintaining an adequate level of mental resilience. Thus, a good burnout strategy takes into account both the physical and the mental components of resilience.

Resilience, or the law of the stimulative arrears

....

FROM ZERO TO ZARA

Exactly two months after Amancio Ortega was born, all hell broke loose. The year was 1936, and in Spain it marked the commencement of the bloodiest war the country had ever seen. For the Ortega family, the outbreak of the Spanish Civil War meant that they would have to flee their home in the small mountain village Busdongo de Arbas. Together with hundreds of rural families, they left for the city in hopes of finding work. After several difficult years, Ortega senior found a job on the railroad in La Coruña. It was hardly enough to feed four hungry children, so Mrs. Ortega supplemented the family's income by working as a housemaid.

When Amancio was thirteen, he walked home with his mother one evening after a long day at work. They stopped at the local grocer's and there Amancio overheard a conversation that would change his life. He heard his mother pleading for credit, while the shop clerk insisted: "No, señora, this time you have to pay." At that moment Amancio – at least, according to well-informed sources, because he himself never gives interviews – decided to get a job and never go to school again. The very next week he was an errand boy and shirt-folder at a local sewing workshop.

Several months later, World War II broke out. No, it certainly wasn't written in the stars that 50 years later,

Amancio Ortega would be one of the most successful people in the world. The life story of the man behind Zara, Massimo Dutti, Bershka and Oysho reads like a fairy tale. From a cash-strapped worker's son to the richest man in Spain, the richest man in the fashion world, and until recently one of the three richest people in the whole world. The Spanish have dubbed his story "From Zero to Zara" – in other words, from rags to riches. For many, Amancio Ortega is the personification of success. His story is far from unique. Just think of former US president Barack Obama, raised by a single mother. Or Nelson Mandela, who spent twenty years in jail, or the orphan Steve Jobs, or single mother J.K. Rowling, or former drug-world errand boy Jay-Z. It is the main theme of countless novels, films and fairy tales; it is the American Dream and the hope of millions.

POST-TRAUMATIC GROWTH

The success of the "rags-to-riches" genre has a lot to do with the perception of the general public that these stories are highly exceptional. And in a sense they are. Unfortunately, in reality, few people who grow up in poverty or live precariously can become superstars. Conversely, there does seem to be an observable link: people who are extraordinarily successful have often had to overcome many obstacles. The British psychologist John Nicholson conducted years of interviews with successful people and came to the conclusion that they all had the same thing in common: at one time or another (usually fairly early in life), they succeeded in fighting their way out of extremely difficult personal and professional incidents.

Could it be that the success in these stories is not "in spite of disaster" but "because of disaster"? That there is a causal relationship between misfortune and success? Charles Dickens, the literary godfather of the rags-to-riches genre, formulated an answer in his novel *Great Expectations*: "Suffering has been stronger than all other teaching...I have been bent and broken, but – I hope – into a better shape."

Not limited to literature, the phenomenon occurs in all different shapes and forms. "Never waste a perfectly good crisis," as Winston Churchill put it. And indeed, some of the biggest companies in the world owe their current success to a crisis in the past. Samsung Electronics, for example, was close to bankruptcy in 1990 (after 20 years at the top in Korea) when manager Lee Kun-Hee had to come up with a crisis plan. That plan made Samsung a world leader in high-tech electronics. Nestlé was a small Swiss company that dealt in powdered milk until World War I, after which they grew into one of the largest food companies in the world. The German brothers Karl and Theo Albrecht were only trying to survive a period of scarcity just after World War II when they came up with the concept of what would later become supermarket chain Aldi. Fifty years ago, the "Asian tigers" (Hong Kong, Singapore, South Korea and Taiwan) were among the poorest countries in the world.

And it turns out to be more than just an economic phenomenon. The Dutch historian Jan Romein already described in 1937 how, in history, a "law of the handicap of the head start" seemed to oppose a "law of the stimulative arrears." In his influential essay on the dialectics of progress, he cites the example of street lighting in London. While many cities already had electric street lighting,

London still used old-fashioned gas lamps. The explanation is simple. In the 19th century, London was one of the most prosperous cities in the world and one of the first to have the budget to introduce street lighting. At the time, gas was a logical choice. Other cities that were only able to introduce street lighting later could opt for a newer technology – electricity. In London, then, we may speak of an "inhibiting head start": they were the first to have the money and the opportunity to install street lighting, but were in the end saddled with an obsolete technology, while other cities, which started with a lag, had much more advanced street lighting.

Ethically, periods of adversity also provided great leaps forward. The recognition of universal human rights received enormous impetus from the horrors of World War II. The most brilliant art is created from lack. Think of Frida Kahlo or Vincent van Gogh. The greatest discoveries are born of necessity, such as the discovery of America by Christopher Columbus. The most beautiful music emerges from pain and sorrow.

And then there is also psychology. There, too, the phenomenon of growth through crisis is well known. Only it's known as "PTG," or "post-traumatic growth."

THE HERALD RESEARCH TEAM

Since the 1960s, extensive research has been done into the consequences of psychological trauma through confrontation with violence, abuse, disaster or illness. In the 1980s, post-traumatic stress disorder (PTSD) was also identified as a condition. Unfortunately, so much attention went to its treatment that research into the other side of the coin was diluted. Nevertheless, only a minority (between eight and 30 percent) of the people who experience a trauma develop PTSD. The great majority recover quickly from the trauma and a significant portion (varying between 30 and 70 percent) seem to experience positive development afterward.

Professor Stephen Joseph of the University of Nottingham described the phenomenon of PTG on the occasion of the *Herald of Free Enterprise* disaster in 1987, when a ferry capsized on the North Sea near Belgium and 193 passengers died. For around 500 of the survivors, the experience in some cases of waiting hours to be rescued from the ice-cold water was particularly traumatic.

Therefore, a Herald Research Team was established at the Institute of Psychiatry to monitor the victims for symptoms of PTSD for several years. Although many of the survivors did indeed exhibit stress-related ailments, Professor Stephen Joseph also noticed that some of the victims actually seemed to be doing remarkably well after the disaster. After three years, he asked all the survivors this question: "Has your view of life changed in a good or in a bad sense since the disaster?" Forty-six percent answered negatively, 43 percent positively.

For some people, Professor Joseph later explained in his book *What Doesn't Kill Us*, trauma leads to greater psychological well-being. People who experience PTG, or post-traumatic growth, are more content with themselves, have a broader perspective on life and also enjoy their social relationships more intensely. The trauma seems to be a sort of catalyst for positive change, in which someone's perspective and inner strength are significantly altered. Joseph adds that this does not necessarily mean that they are also happier.

Fortunately, very few people in the world experience a disaster of this magnitude. The chance that we will be confronted with loss and pain in our lives, however, is close to 100 percent. It can be a divorce or death, a professional failure or natural disaster. Even in the safest countries in the world, the question is not "if" we will experience calamity in our lives, but "when" and "how."

We can be almost sure that something will happen to us. But however bad it is, all traumas also offer a chance for growth and success. The question is: What determines whether a trauma upsets or improves a person's life?

In this context, consider this short notice that appeared in the newspaper several months after the MH17 flight from Amsterdam to Kuala Lumpur crashed in the Ukraine (in July 2014). All 283 passengers on the flight died: *"After the indescribable grief and loss of his daughter Erla, son-in-law Robert, and grandchildren Merel and Mark in the disaster during the Malaysia Airlines flight, it is with great sorrow that we inform you that Henk Palm has died at the age of 93."*

Died of grief. Losing your child is without doubt one of the worst things that can happen to you, and yes, it can be fatal. But what about the family of Ali, a Malaysian PhD student in the Netherlands, who was killed in the same disaster. Did his parents feel the same way? That they would die of grief? Instead, after the death of their beloved son they decided to follow his advice: they planned a family trip to Rotterdam to get to know Ali's world. Later, I read that the parents of 21-year-old Kristina, who was on the same flight, found their daughter's "bucket list" (a list of things you definitely want to do before you die) and wanted to finish it for her.

RESILIENCE GIVES YOU WINGS

Why does one person succumb to his grief, while another draws strength from it? Why does one lie down despondently while the other fights back? Henk Palm's age was certainly an important factor in his death. And Ali's parents had other children to distract them from the event. But these factors are not sufficient to explain why one drowns and the other learns to swim.

The difference in these situations lies in ourselves. Resilience, the ability to rebound when life gets us down, determines how well we can withstand a crisis. Resilience is capable of deflecting all that life dumps on you. And if life drops you like a brick, resilience enables you to bounce back like a rubber ball. It determines not only whether we can survive a crisis, but also whether we will grow as a result.

We know that we will face setbacks in life. People who are successful seem at first glance to be people who always have the wind at their backs. But in practice, what they have in common is that they didn't let a strong headwind beat them back; they learned from their negative experiences. Resilient people succeed like no others in turning every disadvantage into an advantage. Success is not about dealing with positive events, but about dealing with negative events. Resilience gives you the ability to convert bad experiences into wings.

The good news is that our ability to rebound, in contrast to intelligence or character, is only partly determined by our genes. This doesn't mean that we always have a good grasp of it. After all, we cannot choose the traumas we will experience in life. But we can increase our resilience to the extent that we can better withstand those shocks. Compare it to warming up your muscles before you go jogging.

RESILIENCE BRINGS ENGAGEMENT

Research on post-traumatic growth shows very clearly the importance of resilience in times of crisis. In the current brain crisis, resilience is in my opinion the one characteristic we need to invest in, both as a society and as individuals. If burnout stands on one side of the resilience scale, the promise of engagement stands on the other.

More and more researchers agree that engagement is the closest thing to what we might call an "antidote" to burnout. Professor Arnold Bakker of Erasmus University Rotterdam has spent much of his career studying engagement. Together with Wilmar Schaufeli at the University of Utrecht, he worked out the "Utrecht Work Engagement Scale" (UWES), which is now used worldwide as the reference for measuring engagement at work. Bakker identifies three characteristics one must possess in sufficient measure in order to be enthusiastic. These three characteristics are vitality – when someone is full of energy; dedication – when there is a positive attitude towards work; and absorption – when someone is completely involved with work and forgets everything around them.

In his research, he discovered how engaged employees are lively and enthusiastic, full of self-confidence and able to give their lives direction. Through their positive attitude as well as their high activity level, enthusiastic employees create their own positive feedback in the form of esteem, recognition and success. Since the UWES was developed in Utrecht in 2000, the research firm Gallup (among others) has conducted research on the prevalence of engagement. While burnout figures are climbing alarmingly high, the figures for engagement have remained stable for nearly 20 years. Worldwide, some 13 percent of employees are enthusiastic. In the United States, this figure is notably higher at 32 percent. What is striking is that enthusiastic people are also really engaged outside working hours. Of course they sometimes get tired, but they describe their fatigue as a pleasant state because they have a sense of achievement.

CREATING ENGAGEMENT

For many it might seem too good to be true. This sort of enthusiasm is often written off as an addiction. And most people can't stand "workaholics." Bakker's research shows, however, that engaged employees are not addicted to their work. Workaholics feel an inner urge to work hard and don't know how to stop. Engaged people work because they like it, but also enjoy doing other things besides working in their free time. The difference might seem small, but its effect is big: a work addiction leads directly to burnout, while engagement leads you away from it.

Just as burnout arises from a combination of context and personality, engagement is also born of the interplay between the two. On the work floor (the context), autonomy, feedback and a good social network are good predictors of engagement. On a personal level, extraversion, emotional stability and conscientiousness influence engagement. A proactive personality also has a positive link to engagement. People with such personalities intentionally turn their environment to their advantage. They identify opportunities, take action and carry on until they see meaningful change.

Bakker talks about "job crafters": people who actively seek out challenges, consciously apply themselves to learning new things and freely volunteer for projects. They strive for goals because those goals fit within their personal interests and not because other people say they should. For example, a management assistant can make it her responsibility to show new employees around the office even though it is not explicitly part of her job. Job crafters also look for help when they need it and ask for feedback. An employee can actively request feedback from colleagues; that way he can do his job even better.

Engagement is thus a fixed quantity to a certain extent, but fortunately there are variable personality traits that also play a role in its creation. Resilience – the interplay of optimism, effectiveness, stress-resistance and self-esteem – is not inborn, as are other personality traits (such as extraversion). Resilience can be learned. To the extent that employees become more skilled in these traits, they also make more frequent use of work-related resources. Of these regular feedback, social support among colleagues, a variety of skills and opportunities for development are the most important. According to Bakker, investing in variable "personal resources" offers the greatest protection against burnout.

But engagement is more than just an antidote to burnout, and only seeing it in this context is a missed opportunity. From Bakker's research it appears that engaged employees are not only happier and more enthusiastic, but they also have better physical health, such as healthy heart activity. One possible reason for this link is that engaged employees are more likely to participate in relaxing activities that distract them from their work, such as sports, social activities and hobbies. This energy enables them to concentrate better on their work. Moreover, engaged employees have a positive influence not only on themselves, but also on the lives of those around them. They contribute unconsciously to the engagement of their colleagues and are often at the root of innovation and creativity in the workplace, so that the company itself also experiences the positive results.

An American study found that engaged employees are 27 percent less likely to indulge in absenteeism and that the productivity of engaged employees is 18 percent higher on average than that of non-engaged employees. A study conducted by the Dutch government concerning sustainable employability calculated that a 1 percent increase in productivity among Dutch employees would yield 6 billion euros a year. For a company with 100 employees, that translates into an annual revenue increase of 95,000 euros.

As if all those advantages and potential profit margins were not convincing enough, engagement also happens to be the greatest predictor of "flow." This state was identified by the American psychologist Mihaly Csikszentmihalyi as a mental state in which a person is completely absorbed in his or her activity, such that all space, time and surrounding events seem to disappear. It is the highest state of focus and motivation in which all negative emotions disappear and one is completely involved in what one is doing.

Flow is much more than just a pleasant feeling. Flow is an accelerator for resilience. Csikszentmihalyi's research shows that flow not only makes people happier, it also makes them more successful. This is not illogical if you consider that flow is the ultimate state for processing new knowledge and driving up production. The more moments of flow employees attain, the more productive they become, enabling them to have more moments of flow, and so on.

A world-renowned example of flow is the painting of the Sistine Chapel by Michelangelo. It is said that the artist was so completely absorbed in his work that he did not sleep, eat or drink until he collapsed from exhaustion. When the work was finished, he was supposedly nearly blind due to the amount of paint that had dribbled into his eyes over the years.

But you don't have to be a world-famous painter to experience flow. Most people have had such an experience at some point. It is often associated with sports, music, meditation and art, but moments of flow are possible in every profession. The great frustration for many is that they can't summon flow whenever they want to. Here, too, the answer lies in strengthening resilience.

ON TOP OF THE PYRAMID

Investing in resilience isn't just a source of opportunities at work. The concept also touches on the most basic human needs. One of the first areas that scientific psychology tried to map out was exactly that: What constitutes the basis of human well-being?

Abraham Maslow made his reputation in the 1940s with his world-famous "pyramid of human needs," which connects intrinsic human motivation with a hierarchy of needs. At the very base of the pyramid are bodily needs, followed by the need for safety, social contact and esteem. At the very top is self-actualization. The idea is that bodily needs must be met first before a human being will try to fulfill the "higher" needs. To put it simplistically: first you look for food, then for a roof over your head, and only then will you have time to make and maintain friendships.

Maslow's pyramid has been sharply criticized over the years because in practice it turns out that the "lower" needs do not always have to be fulfilled before you strive for the "higher" ones. Nevertheless, we see that resilient people usually tick all the boxes until they reach the top. In life, this is the best place to be: on top of Maslow's pyramid. And thanks to science, the way to the top is increasingly more accessible. A well-known pronouncement of the American psychologist Daniel Gilbert in this regard is: "Soon (psychological) science will be able to tell us exactly how to get what we want in life, but it will never be able to tell us what life we want. That will always be our decision."

Science can tell us a great deal about the way we can realize our ambitions, but the decision to do so will always be ours. It is a question of seizing the opportunities we are offered and insisting on opportunities where possible. And that is as true for individuals, companies and organizations as it is for society.

At the top of the pyramid shines not only the promise of resilience, which among other things protects against burnout and stress, but also the promise of happiness. It may seem far-fetched, but it's not. Happiness today is more within reach than ever. I discovered this myself, in spite of my initial skepticism, in a Swiss mountain village.

HAPPINESS IN THE SCANNER

I met "the happiest person in the world" a few years ago in the heart of the Alps. The sophisticated town of Davos is perennially popular with skiers and hikers, but once a year it's transformed into a heavily guarded and exclusive meeting place so that the business lunch of the world can take place: the World Economic Forum. Heads of state and government leaders, the crème de la crème of international corporate life, leading thinkers, renowned artists and prominent scientists gather to discuss recent global developments and challenges. As a young scientist, I had the honor of attending this conference in 2012. The session that made my scientific heart beat faster was entitled "The Science and Art of Happiness." Each speaker discussed "happiness" from his or her own perspective.

Daniel Goleman (known for his bestseller on emotional intelligence) moderated the conversation between John Kabat-Zinn (the father of mindfulness), Tania Singer (who has conducted groundbreaking research on empathy), Richard Davidson (known for his research on neuroplasticity) and several other highly placed guests. Every single one of them a pioneer in his or her discipline, debating the subject of happiness. That I had to see.

The session took place in one of the smaller rooms of the conference hall. That seemed logical to me. I suspected it would be mainly a "white badge" session. In Davos, the invitees wear blue badges, their significant others wear white ones, and every year a few activities are also organized for the "white badges." I thought I would be one of the few blue badges at the session. "The leaders of the world surely have more urgent business to attend to," I thought.

I was badly mistaken. There was room for a hundred people. When I arrived, spectators were plastered against the walls and people were starting to sit on the carpet. When the session started, we were packed in like sardines. Blue badges mingled with white badges. Happiness, as I then understood for the first time, is everybody's business.

There are no categories of people who want happiness. It doesn't depend on your age, social class, function or ideology: happiness is the ultimate goal for us all. The other goals we pursue, the money we earn, the business we transact, the success we reap, the trips we take: the promise of happiness lurks behind every one of our ambitions.

Happiness is not only the ultimate goal, it also seems unattainable to most people. It's Godot never arriving. It's the discovery of heaven. The best that we as human beings can hope for is that we are not too unhappy on the way to that unattainable happiness. At least, that's what I thought before the session began.

And then he entered, "the happiest person in the world." With his red-orange robe, bald head and ear-to-ear smile, Matthieu Ricard looked as if he had run away from a Buddhist monastery. He walked around glowing the whole time, as if he had just swallowed a ball of gold. Not my type, if you really want to know. Much too merry to be credible, I thought, far too woolly. Until he started talking.

He began: "What is happiness, or should we call it 'well-being' instead? Because, of course, happiness is no more than an agreeable feeling. It is a deep sensation of serenity and satisfaction, a state in which all emotions can be present. Even grief."

Not a bad definition, it seemed to me. And not at all woolly. I glanced at the program to look at this man's profile. "PhD in cellular genetics, confidant of the Dalai Lama, doing research on Buddhism for 40 years." And he wasn't finished yet:

"But how do we go about our quest for happiness these days? We often look outside ourselves. Unfortunately our control of the outside world is limited, temporary and often even imaginary. If we turn inward, we quickly notice that we have a better chance. Is it not the mind that translates our experiences in the outside world into joy or sorrow?"

Then Ricard went into the way in which we can make our minds more sensitive to happiness in practice, and that was according to him (hardly surprising, coming from a monk) through meditation: "A manner of transforming the mind so that it absorbs happiness instead of rejecting it." I looked in the direction of neuroscientist Richard Davidson. How would he react to this assertion? And indeed, he took the floor.

Davidson explained that he had tested Ricard's assertion by having him meditate daily in an MRI scanner at the University of Wisconsin-Madison. It must have been very uncomfortable for Ricard to meditate in a big tube with 128 sensors on his head. But the results were astonishing. While he was meditating on compassion, the strongest gamma rays ever measured in neuroscience were registered. Gamma rays are associated with heightened awareness, alert functioning and a supreme state of happiness. Since then, Ricard has been known as the "happiest person in the world."

There are many things you can take away from Ricard's scan experiment. He himself emphasized how meditation has a powerful effect on neuroplasticity, the biological variability of our brains. But personally what I remembered was the following: happiness is not just a desire, it is attainable, moreover measurable, and it does indeed reside within.

THE SCIENTIFIC SEARCH FOR HAPPINESS

Over the years, science has jumped on the bandwagon in the search for happiness. If psychology was until recently committed mainly to the reduction of human suffering, today the big question is how science can contribute to increasing human happiness. In light of this increased interest, Rotterdam professor emeritus Ruut Veenhoven decided several years ago to start up a "Database of Happiness," a database that now holds more than 9,000 scientific publications on happiness.

Research on happiness has grown to the extent that it appears to be too big to comprehend. However, several neurological scientists at University College London succeeded in combining scientific research on the "resources of happiness" into a compact mathematical formula that predicts happiness. The formula was tested with both fMRI scans and surveys and the findings were published in the authoritative scientific journal *Proceedings of the National Academy of Sciences*. The formula is:

$$\text{HAPPINESS } (t) = w_0 + w_1 \sum_{j=1}^{t} \gamma^{t-j} CR_j + w_2 \sum_{j=1}^{t} \gamma^{t-j} EV_j + w_3 \sum_{j=1}^{t} \gamma^{t-j} RP_j$$

Happiness = basic mood (w_0) + what you're satisfied with (CR) + what you get on average (EV) + the difference between what you get on average and what you get now (RPE). The recurring Σ functions weigh each factor based on recent history.

To summarize, this formula teaches us that we are happy if something exceeds our expectations. In that sense, the formula confirms what many thinkers, writers and philosophers already knew. A famous quote on the subject from Stephen Hawking, the brilliant physicist who has suffered from the neurological disease ALS since his youth, is: "My expectations were reduced to zero when I turned 21. Everything since then has been a bonus."

In addition to the importance of the unexpected as an aspect of happiness, this formula makes clear that happiness is mainly determined in practice by a subtle interplay of the constant and the temporary, on the one hand, and by the inner and the outer, on the other. On the inside, we can distinguish emotional, psychological and mental factors. We can tinker with these factors in order to exploit our mental resilience. I will explore this in more depth in part II.

PART II

PROFITING FROM RESILIENCE

We all have mental capital. Some people's startup capital is greater than others, but those with the greatest advantage do not always reap the biggest profits. That too has to do with the law of the stimulative arrears. That capital helps us through life and determines how resilient we are.

Each of us has the ability to make the most of his or her life. The choice of whether to squander or redeem our mental startup capital lies with us. For some, this means little more than adopting a positive attitude towards life; for others, it means working hard to increase their own resilience. Regardless of where you start, investing in mental capital is a risk-free investment. You can only profit from it.

You don't become more mentally resilient overnight. It is a choice that you make and requires two decisions. The first is the decision to play an active role in your own life, and the second is to feel and take responsibility. Both sound more logical and easier than they are in practice.

All too often, we let ourselves be swept along by what happens to us. We like to immerse ourselves in a bath of self-pity and, at the same time, we usually prefer to blame others. What we too often overlook is that how things turn out doesn't really depend on whose fault it is and what a pity it is that it happened at all. Life comes as it comes. But it is still our life and the only way to change something about it is by being more proactive. If we don't want others to determine what direction we take, then we must take control ourselves. Even if that means a hefty portion of rebellion is needed.

If you want a better mind, you have to want to take hold of your life. It's not enough to make a few New Year's resolutions on January 1 that gradually fade over time. You have to actively set yourself achievable goals and arrange your life so that you can achieve them. Take time to think about your dreams and expectations, because maybe you've neglected something that's very important to you.

Resilient people learn from negative events and actively seek out new opportunities. Within themselves, with others, in their surroundings and in the outside world. They are also not afraid to accept help and actively seek out resources. They make connections out of strength, joy and hope and this yields benefits on several levels: mental, psychological, social, financial, economic, societal – you name it.

As an individual, you will have to roll up your sleeves and get to work if you want to increase your mental capital. This also applies to companies: unless they make an effort, it is impossible to make the mental capital of their employees grow. Unfortunately, many executives – even in the midst of the current burnout crisis – are very reluctant to invest actively in their mental capital and that of their employees, because it takes time, money and energy. Even the recognition of burnout as a occupational illness has still not changed things much. In the corporate world and in the media, the debate gets hung up on the question of who is to blame for the current burnout epidemic. Is it the companies that urgently need to change? Is the government responsible? Or does the cause lie with the employees themselves? It's interesting to conduct this discussion in a nuanced way, but the answer will always be somewhere in the middle. Employers, employees and the government will have to change together. Each bears part of the responsibility. Let us focus primarily on how we can solve the problem, and not so much on who has caused the problem and to what extent.

Fortunately, some companies want to take on the current burnout crisis by investing in resilience. And this has been fruitful. Not only for the employees, but also for the companies themselves. A positive brain strategy ensures that employees perform better and are less likely to call in sick, but by adopting a brain-friendly strategy, the frontrunners in terms of resilience also attract the best and brightest minds. As an upcoming talent, which company would you choose? The company that offers high wages and serious material advantages, but few opportunities for further development and a high risk of burnout? Or the company that in addition to material advantages also offers the chance to grow and increase your mental resilience?

Choosing to invest in mental capital is the first step. But then comes the hard part: getting started. Most people and companies have only a vague idea of what resilience actually means. All too often I see well-meaning attempts fail because they are not embedded in a broader vision or because the measures taken counteract one another. To enhance resilience, we first have to find the resources that will help us jump higher. What characteristics ensure that we bounce back when life gets us down? What drives resilience? This is what we will be looking at in this part of the book.

An important point: the tools for mental resilience are within us. Self-control or willpower gives us the strength of motivation. Consciously engaging with our consciousness and unconscious is the second tool, and ensures that we can reduce the negative effects of stress considerably. With focus, we can increase our cognitive intelligence. And finally, we can appeal to and stimulate our optimistic ur-instinct to provide the emotional basis for cashing in on mental capital.

Don't think about the marshmallow

The value of self-control

. . . .

WHAT MAKES A GENIUS TICK

Leonardo da Vinci, Mozart and Einstein. Each in their own way changed the world. Each in their own way has made sure that we still remember them dozens or even hundreds of years later. But what do they actually have in common? Why did they, and not their colleagues and friends, end up in the history books?

Many will say "intelligence" or "talent." We like to believe in the power and exceptional abilities of the individual. Studies show, however, that only 25 percent of a person's success can be attributed to intelligence or innate talent. What explains the other 75 percent? Is it chance, luck or perhaps intervention from above that actualizes a person's genius?

Einstein himself explained his success by pointing to his extraordinary curiosity. He said: "I have no special talent. I am only passionately curious." He was, however, strongly convinced of the power of imagination. Einstein did not have a brilliant academic career, but believed that fairy tales had shaped his intelligence. "Logic will get you from A to Z; imagination will take you everywhere," he said. Wolfgang Amadeus Mozart saw it otherwise: "Neither a lofty intelligence, nor imagination, nor both together go to making a genius. Love, love, love: that is the soul of genius." In a famous passage from his diary, the child prodigy describes how an entire symphony sprang from his head in one night. Leonardo da Vinci looked at it from yet another angle: "One can have no smaller or greater mastery than mastery of oneself."

For each genius – how could it be otherwise – there is an explanation for his or her success, but the American psychologist Angela Lee Duckworth was the first to actually research the question. She dove into the biographies of 300 "actualized geniuses" and looked for what they all had in common: the quality that made the difference in comparison to the rest. This is how she formulated the first well-founded answer to the question humanity has been asking itself since the age of Homer: "What makes the great great?" The distinguishing feature is called "grit."

GRIT MAKES THE DIFFERENCE

Duckworth discovered that geniuses always have two recurring qualities. The most obvious common denominator was the tendency not to give up in the face of adversity. Also crucial was the inclination to seek out new challenges. All 300 actualized geniuses had invested at least ten years of their lives in a particular project or talent before reaching the top. They were obsessed, even if it seemed like things weren't going well for a little while (or a long time).

Duckworth called the combination of the two characteristics "grit": the ability to withstand challenges for a very long time. And in every case it turned out to be more decisive than genius. A famous example of the "greatest" not always being the most brilliant is Maria Anna Mozart, the sister of Amadeus, who according to some sources possessed even greater talent than her brother, but since she was a girl, it was not considered appropriate for her to perform at the major venues of the time. Charles Darwin corresponded regularly with his cousin Francis Galton, who was widely regarded as intellectually superior to Darwin. The term "nature versus nurture," for example, can be ascribed not to Darwin but to Galton. But it was Darwin who obsessively devoted his life to the study of evolution.

Many "greats" recognized how indebted they were to certain of their contemporaries. Another constant is that they often admitted that their talent was not so extraordinary, but that their "grit" was the real reason for their success – although they didn't call it that. After the passage in his diary about the nighttime symphony inspiration, Mozart described how he then spent months elaborating and refining a composition that was essentially already inside his head. Einstein said: "It's not that I'm so smart, I just stay with problems longer." Grit. And Da Vinci wrote: "Learning never exhausts the mind." Grit.

Duckworth's analysis focused exclusively on historical figures, but you could probably find a few examples of grit in your own environment. I remember the following quote from Will Smith, who has enjoyed massive success as a rapper, actor, producer and businessman. Asked for the secret of his success, he said: "The only thing that I see that is distinctly different about me is that I'm not afraid to die on a treadmill. I will not be out-worked, period. You might have more talent than me, you might be smarter than me, you might be sexier than me, you might be all those things you got it on me in nine categories. but if we get on a treadmill together, there's two things: you're getting off first, or I'm going to die. It's really that simple."

After her discovery, Angela Lee Duckworth continued to investigate the "grit theory," also among less well-known people. She developed a grit test of just 12 questions and presented them to everyone she could think of. Among her students, gaming champions and soldiers in training, the grit test appeared to be a better predictor of success than all other entrance exams, intelligence tests and endurance tests. Other researchers also began working with grit and collected additional proof that grit not only has an effect on the life of the person in question, but also on the people around them. Teachers with grit help their students perform better in a given subject, and also to enjoy more success later in life.

Although grit research is still in its infancy, it is abundantly clear that investing in this characteristic can have an enormous impact on corporate life. Think of job applications, which, for lack of anything better, are largely judged on the basis of diplomas and experience. With a well-stocked CV, you currently stand a better chance of making a good impression. But according to grit theory, you should judge candidates more positively who have been working at something for a longer period, and therefore perhaps have a less diversified background. They might have more grit than someone who goes in search of new challenges after a couple of years.

Another area in which grit can cause a big stir in business is management. If a teacher with grit can ensure that his students enjoy greater success, what impact does an executive's grit have on his staff? Instead of making executives attend courses on "customer satisfaction" and "motivation training," it should suffice to increase the manager's own grit quotient. The question is: Is it possible? Can you give someone "grit" or cultivate it?

Grit research is still young, but it's gradually becoming clearer what its basic components are. These are: (1) the ability to think long term and (2) the ability to control one's own behavior. Both together in an area of psychology that is better known than grit: research on self-control.

Self-control is not a precondition for grit, but the two are closely related. People with self-control are better able to resist daily temptations because they can better estimate the long-term impact. People who can control their daily behavior score higher on the grit test. One important difference between grit and self-control is the perception surrounding them. For many, grit seems too abstract to be a priority objective, but self-control? That seems plausible. And we try again every year.

THE FIRST SUNDAY IN JANUARY

Every first Sunday in January, there they are: the joggers in the park. In the early hours of the morning, they brave the winter cold to work themselves into a sweat and start the year out right. This year, you hear them thinking with every slap of their sport shoes, this year I'm really doing it. But then come the New Year's receptions and the winter blues and the spring fever and the April showers and before you even have time to think that maybe you should start jogging too, the park is once again blissfully calm and empty on Sunday morning.

New Year's resolutions are an excellent example of the fact that will alone is not enough to reach a goal. However strong your willpower might be, and however great your self-confidence, to turn your dreams into reality you need something besides willpower. That something is self-control, the ability to control and modify your emotions, responses and behavior patterns when you think it's necessary.

Naturally we as human beings like to believe that we have self-control. That we decide who we are, what we do and how we order our lives. Free will is the most beautiful illusion that we as humans cherish. Until we fall hopelessly in love. Or fall prey to an addiction. Or just can't seem to lose those last few pounds. When we fight back our tears. In such moments we feel helpless, because we are confronted with the fact that we don't have as much self-control as we'd like.

Self-control ensures that people do not always give in to their impulses, that they can decide to do the right thing or the smart thing instead of just letting themselves be carried along by emotions and instinct. The ability to control impulses is crucial, both in daily life and at decisive moments (such as a crisis), to our quality of life. It prevents us from spending money on frivolities and enables us to think long term. It ensures that we don't gobble down sweets every day or waste precious hours surfing on the Internet. Self-control stands between us and addiction, obesity and destructive behavior. But if self-control is so good for us, why don't we have more of it? And if we agree that we don't have enough self-control, is there some way we can develop it?

The man who first put self-control on the psychological map was the American researcher Walter Mischel. In 1970, he conducted the legendary marshmallow experiments, in which he tested toddlers for self-control by leaving them alone for 15 minutes with a marshmallow. The children were promised that if they hadn't eaten the marshmallow in that time, they would get a second one. Only a small minority made no attempt to wait. One-third of the approximately 600 children tested succeeded in leaving the marshmallow alone for the entire 15 minutes.

Age appears to be the most determining factor in self-control. This is because self-control is found in the anterior prefrontal cortex, which is the part of the brain that develops last. Studies show that the prefrontal cortex is only fully developed between the ages of 20 and 25. Thus, children have less self-control than adults. A second important determinant was the situation at home. Children from broken families were found to give in to temptation much faster than children who grew up with both parents.

The most groundbreaking results were only discovered 20 years later during a follow-up study. When the participants in the marshmallow experiment were re-examined, it seemed that the children who earned a second marshmallow had done much better in life than those who had eaten the first. Those who had demonstrated more self-control in the past had become adults who had better physical and mental health, struggled with fewer addictions, had less contact with crime, enjoyed greater academic success and on average earned more money.

Recent studies confirm this: the degree of self-control in childhood predicts physical and mental health in adulthood. Particularly striking is a New Zealand study in which twins were followed for 27 years. Despite a shared family background, those with less self-control during childhood were also those who had poorer health, more financial problems and were involved in more criminal activities in their thirties.

At first glance, these results might seem demotivating. They seem to suggest that self-control is innate and that those who have the misfortune to be born without it are doomed to fail in life. The savvy observer, however, will understand that Mischel's research also contains good news: the marshmallow experiment suggests that innate intelligence or social status is less decisive for success than self-control. This hypothesis was later elaborated by Nobel Prize winner James Heckman at the University of Chicago, and forms the basis of Angela Lee Duckworth's grit analysis.

SELF-CONTROL CAN BE LEARNED

Several studies prove that self-control can, in fact, be learned. In the brain, the ability to control your impulses runs primarily through three specific parts of the prefrontal cortex: the dorsolateral prefrontal cortex (the executive part of the brain), the ventromedial prefrontal cortex (where emotional control is located) and the cortex cingularis anterior (the area that processes pain). Not coincidentally, these are also the areas where it is thought that intelligence develops. This seems to correspond to the general perception: people that exhibit a great deal of self-control are usually described as "wise" because they "think before they act." In part, self-control, like intelligence, is determined by biological predestination, via the genes.

But that is certainly not the end of the story. Our brain is much more malleable than we often believe. We are literally never too old to learn, and this is also true of our behavior. But that other old cliché is also true: a good start is half the battle, and good habits formed when young make all the difference.

The children in the marshmallow experiment were between the ages of four and six. Self-control is one of the most important predictors for success later in life, but also one of the last things to develop in the human brain. On average, we learn self-control around the age of five, although there are children who do so earlier.

One of the first ways parents notice that their baby is beginning to become more sensible and learning to control his impulses is by playing hide and seek. It's one of the first games parents can play with their baby. Mom and dad hide behind a chair or a blanket and reappear somewhere else. Parents and babies alike are crazy about it. At nine months, a baby looks away from the place you were last seen. In other words, the baby controls the impulse to always look in the same place, but begins to understand that he will have more success if he also looks somewhere else.

The fun really begins when the roles are reversed. At some point, toddlers decide that they want to hide too. The first time, the search is usually over quite quickly: as soon as mom or dad enters the room, the toddler leaps into view with enthusiasm. At such moments, he or she is not yet able to exercise patience. The next time, the toddler will not jump into view but will betray his or her presence by giggling uncontrollably or calling out: "You can't find me!" Only when you play the game regularly will the child get better at finding a hiding place, and also develop the ability to control her own desire to be found by you. Playing hide and seek with your child is essentially a way of teaching her to control her impulses, but in a very pleasant way.

DELAYED GRATIFICATION

Of course, playing hide and seek isn't all that's needed to promote self-control in children. A healthy diet and sufficient sleep are important prerequisites for healthy development, including development of the brain. Just think how well you can control yourself if you haven't slept enough, or when you go to the supermarket hungry. The example set by parents is also important in terms of self-control. This is one of the reasons why addiction is passed on from generation to generation.

But the decisive factor is bonding between parent and child. Children who feel safe can control their behavior considerably earlier and better. The importance of consistent upbringing for the development of self-control was also shown during a follow-up study to the marshmallow experiment. This time, the toddlers were divided into two groups. The researchers promised new pencils to both groups in the waiting room. The first group received them after only a few minutes. The second group was not given pencils at all. Then the children were subjected to the marshmallow test.

The difference between the two groups was immense. The children in the second group, who saw the researchers as untrustworthy, on average waited only three minutes before they ate their candy. The children who had received their pencils in the waiting room, and therefore trusted the researchers, waited on average 12 minutes.

Children of parents who regularly make promises that they fail to keep, who frequently change their mind or who make threats that they never carry out, learn at an early age not to believe in the principle of "delayed gratification." They go for "instant fulfillment" because they have no confidence that the real reward is yet to follow. The same goes for teachers whose reactions are unreliable. They usually can't keep control of their class.

The best-known extremes are people who seem to have a different hobby every month because they give up halfway on ever being good at what they do, or adults who constantly indulge in sweets because they're not convinced they will become slim by avoiding them.

IN A VELVET BOX

Good bonding, supported by a safe upbringing, is a basic condition for positive education and development. Because self-control is such a good predictor of success, some parents make an extra effort to encourage this trait by focusing on it to an extreme degree. The unofficial leader of this movement is the American "tiger mom" Amy Chua. This professor of law at Yale University caused parents around the world to bridle with her book *Battle Hymn of a Tiger*

Mom, in which she explains that Chinese mothers are better at bringing up children than Western mothers because they employ strict discipline and stimulate their children's self-control. According to Chua, a Western upbringing is far too focused on self-actualization and "do what you like," to the point that the children (in spite of their socio-economic advantages) systematically underachieve.

Amy Chua was widely criticized because her methods were thought to push today's youth, who are already under great pressure, even further into a corner. Her vision was described as cold and ruthless, but also as counterproductive: by exercising too much parental control over children, you do not stimulate the development of self-control – at best, your children will just listen to you more closely. They perform to please their parents and not themselves. And that, later in life when parental authority falls away, can yield the opposite result.

However, I think there is something to be said about the idea that today's upbringing is not focused enough on self-control. And that parents, educators and schools must take on the important task of paying more attention to it. Not because there is too little involvement or concern, but rather the opposite: because they want to retain too much control. More than ever, children today grow up in a velvet box. They are protected against accidents, bullying, poor school results, illness and grief, get a mobile phone to take to school with them and are picked up from the school entrance. Is it possible that we don't expose our children to enough temptations, so that they don't learn to cope with them until it's too late? And like Pinocchio are drawn to an island of donkeys by the first circus director that comes their way with big promises?

You cannot learn self-control if someone simply comes along and shows you how it should be; you have to embrace and practice it. And that is something you learn by experience and training.

FOUR PRINCIPLES FOR SELF-CONTROL

The way in which self-control is developed in children can teach us a great deal about how we can improve self-control in adults. Because even though the basis for self-control is already established in childhood, you can still make great progress in this area as an adult. Teaching self-control to adults mainly follows the same principles as it does with children. First, there is belief in delayed gratification. The principles of intrinsic motivation, self-regulation through distraction, and the limits of ego depletion also play a role. There are also specific tools for increasing your self-control. We will discuss these further.

PRINCIPLE 1
Delayed gratification

The first and most important way to increase your self-control or that of others is by reinforcing or restoring the belief in long-term reward. Almost everyone has had some experience in life when this confidence was broken. Sometimes through a chance combination of circumstances, sometimes through the conscious actions of particular people. Then we ask ourselves, "Why are we actually doing this?" The more often our faith in delayed gratification is violated, the less we will be inclined to believe in it. The earlier we lose faith in the long term, the more difficult it is to restore that faith.

Drug counseling provides daily examples of this. Addicts seem incapable of being convinced that they can get their life back on the right track by quitting drugs. A bad childhood, in which belief in the future was regularly thwarted, is often (but not always) behind a strong addiction. Counselors often have a difficulty convincing such people that they can improve their lives by staying off drugs. The way to restore their faith in the future is by showing results as quickly as possible.

In the treatment of depression, regaining hope in the future is always the first step. But believing in the future is not only important for those who want to overcome addiction or depression – it's also crucial for people who want to follow a diet or learn a new language. A diet is always easiest to maintain if the pounds are melting away, and learning a language is only pleasant if you can track your progress in conversations.

People who have little confidence in a positive outcome often find it difficult to stick with things. They start on something, but if it doesn't advance fast enough they quit. Such people are also inclined to lower their ambitions to avoid disappointment. This strategy of "self-handicapping" is typical for people with a fear of failure and may be positive in the short run (after all, you avoid disappointment), but in the long run it is usually disadvantageous.

Restoring someone's belief in the future is not easy, but it is certainly not impossible. If it's a question of disease or disorder, therapy can offer a way forward. Incorporating psychological optimism (see p. 116) – for example, Martin Seligman's PERMA model – provides benefits in many cases.

For companies and organizations, it is especially important to help employees believe in the principle of delayed gratification by being consistent. Few things undermine satisfaction and engagement at work like inconsistent personnel policies. Executives who make it clear to their employees that hard work pays will always reap the benefits. But only on the condition that their policy is not contrary to the second principle of self-control: intrinsic motivation.

PRINCIPLE 2

Intrinsic motivation

The second principle of self-control seems at first glance to be the direct opposite of the principle of delayed gratification, and is the difficult-to-accept observation that a system of rewards does not actually work. In fact, the prospect of being rewarded has a pronounced negative effect on our motivation and our ability to learn. Although this principle has been known to psychologists since the 1960s, it has clearly not penetrated the business world. Premiums, bonuses and extras are firmly established in our economy, while research shows that these systems are disastrous for the intrinsic motivation of employees. The same detrimental effect also applies to students and children. Research shows that rewards have only a temporary effect, and do not lead to lasting changes in attitude or behavior. Many studies in social psychology show that people who expect a reward will perform worse than people who expect nothing.

The examples are legion. When people are paid to give blood, fewer candidates show up. Children taking an intelligence test score worse if they are rewarded for each correct answer. Students who receive gifts for their efforts do not perform that well at school, and employees who receive bonuses do not work as hard.

The problem is that rewards undermine your intrinsic motivation. In the first place, it makes performance dependent on reward. Imagine: your boss promises you a reward if your department's revenue increases by 2 percent. Maybe you'll work a bit harder in the coming months, because of course you want to earn a bit more. But such rewards are a double-edged sword. If your boss doesn't provide a premium next time, you might feel were being denied something. Because you got something extra last time, so why not now? The first reward sets a standard for the future, as it were, and if it's repeated often, the recipients will even become fully dependent on it. If there are no more rewards, they will no longer make an effort.

The second reason why rewards don't work is related to the first. Rewards don't work because the gift becomes the most important motivation and replaces the pleasure of working. This difference is most clearly visible among students. Young people who are only studying to get a diploma are less interested in the subject, so they remember less. Their peers who study because the content interests them achieve a state of flow more easily. They're not primarily interested in the results of their study (a diploma); rather, they're motivated by the content. They want to master a discipline because the material fascinates them and are less interested in the final score. Ironically, they usually get better results.

A third reason militating against rewards is that it is a highly transparent form of manipulation. Rewards are in fact concealed threats. If you promise a child that he will

receive candy for finishing his homework, the child under-
stands that he will be punished if he doesn't. Blackmail has
the desired effect over the short term, but in the long run it
sows distrust and suspicion. Intrinsic motivation cannot be
forced – not in the form of punishment and not in the form
of reward.

This basic principle of self-control obviously has far-reach-
ing implications for corporate life. It actually means that
executives should reconsider their personnel policies and
that is not always easy, because their employees may have
become accustomed to a culture of rewards and will doubt-
less protest if the system is suddenly changed. Moreover, research into the negative effects of rewards might be moving
full speed ahead, but at the moment there is no clear vision
of what the positive alternative might be. If you abolish rewards, what do you replace them with?

On this score, science has a long way to go, but there are
a number of interesting proposals out there. As a company,
you can promote a culture of recognition and gratitude instead of focusing on material rewards. Stimulating autonomy is likewise an interesting trajectory. As an individual,
you can also make a difference. Your company might work
with rewards, but you can still look for what intrinsically
motivates you. Does your drive come from positive reactions from clients? Or do you get a kick out of completing
a task on time and within budget? Pay extra attention to
these things. If you also receive a financial reward, that's
great, but don't make it your ultimate goal. In this way, try
actively to keep your self-control up to speed. Look out for
potential pitfalls and adapt accordingly.

I was once hired by the HR manager of a company where a real culture of complaint had arisen when a number of bonuses that had been promised were postponed on account of less-than-favorable economic prospects. In the workplace, people were talking about nothing else. Whatever effort the management team asked of staff, it was tallied up. Every minute of overtime was hotly protested. There was a hostile atmosphere between staff and management. Executives felt their employees only showed up to collect their bonuses and had no consideration for the company's interests.

The entire company was at risk of reaching an impasse. The HR manager reacted by drawing up a clear "personnel handbook" with precise rules on performance and rewards, and when it would be possible to receive a bonus. It was important not only to temper expectations, but also to increase work satisfaction. Emphasis was also placed on increasing the employees' intrinsic motivation – for example, by increasing autonomy. Employees were encouraged to create their own niche and specialize in it. They could decide independently how to reach a particular goal, and management interfered less along the way. The focus was no longer on what the employee achieved, but how.

PRINCIPLE 3
Self-regulation through distraction

The biggest discoveries happen by chance, when you're looking for something completely different. Think of the discovery of America by Christopher Columbus, or the invention of the pacemaker – developed during research on hypothermia. The same is true of research on self-control. With his marshmallows, Mischel wanted to research self-regulation, not self-control: techniques people use to control their emotions and behavior. He deliberately used toddlers as guinea pigs because he wanted to investigate which techniques people used if they are not yet influenced by cultural and social expectations about self-control. To put it simply: he wanted to know what techniques Mother Nature gave us for controlling ourselves, and which ones were most efficient.

Not coincidentally, Mischel's first study focused primarily on the many ways in which the children tried to prevent themselves from eating the marshmallow. He describes how some children kept their hands clapped over their eyes or turned away so as not to have to look at the marshmallow, while others pulled their hair or kicked the table in order not to give in to temptation. Some children even stroked the marshmallow as if it were a stuffed animal.

In general we can distinguish five methods for self-regulation: (1) trying to avoid the situation, (2) trying to change the situation, (3) shifting the attention, (4) adjusting appreciation of the situation, and (5) repressing a reaction. The most successful technique in the marshmallow experiments was shifting the attention through distraction. Children who sang, talked to themselves or crept under the table touched the marshmallow less than all the others.

Self-regulation through distraction works best not only with children who aren't supposed to eat sweets, but is also a known principle in managing the emotions. When we are overcome by rage, grief or fear, temporarily distracting ourselves is the best way to decrease the experience of pain and maintain self-control. This explains, for example, why it's good to do an hour of sports if you're angry. Note: this is a temporary measure. Over the long term, avoiding emotions is negative, period.

Walter Mischel himself made the following blunt statement about coping with romantic disappointment: "After a break-up, take two aspirins and don't complain." A remarkable statement coming from a psychologist, to say the least, but the explanation is obvious: by immediately lessening an emotional experience, it takes less time to process and you are sooner able to look at it from a neutral standpoint.

With the exception of extreme emotions, distraction is also an effective method to prevent worrying. Unwanted thoughts that demand our attention at the most inconvenient times are a plague that many people face. In the next chapter (on consciousness), I will explore in more depth the ways in which we can deal with our wandering thoughts more consciously. For the time being, I will restrict myself to the role that distraction can play in warding off worry.

By consciously focusing your attention on something specific when a worry pops up, the brain will have no choice but to follow. The American psychologist Daniel Wegner described this technique of "focused distraction" in his book *White Bears and Other Unwanted Thoughts*. The method consists in giving your brain a small but focused assignment (for example, counting backwards from 100, doing a crossword puzzle or reading an article). A good illustration of this method is the game in which you're told "not to think of a white bear." Instead of ordering yourself absolutely not to think of a white bear, the solution lies in thinking of a yellow or a green bear.

If you apply the method of "focused distraction" consistently whenever a certain thought comes up, after a while your brain will understand that this thought is no longer important to you. The worrying thought moves to the back of your mind and only appears when you consciously recall it.

Self-regulation through distraction as a technique is particularly useful on the individual level, but organizations and companies can also make use of it. Imagine that a meeting always gets stuck on the same point. It could help to shelve that particular topic and bring up a new agenda point. You could anticipate this and have a new subject ready in case things get stuck. If something negative in the workplace starts taking over your thoughts, take a short time-out. Just going for a walk, meditating or concentrating on your breathing can make a big difference.

PRINCIPLE 4
The limits of ego depletion

One thing that makes it so difficult to achieve self-control is its last principle, "willpower exhaustion" or "ego depletion." This principle was first described by the American psychologist Roy Baumeister, who is best known for his research on willpower. In Florida, Baumeister discovered that people who showed a great deal of self-control when carrying out a specific task showed notably less when carrying out the next task.

Baumeister used several experiments, such as one in which hungry students enter a room in which chocolate cookies have just been baked. One group is left alone and allowed to eat the cookies. The next group is not allowed to touch the fragrant cookies, but are given free access to a plate of radishes. Afterwards, both groups of students must solve an unsolvable puzzle. The second group gives up much more quickly. Apparently they used a lot of their energy trying to resist the tasty cookies and don't have enough willpower to spend a long time concentrating on a tricky puzzle. In another experiment it was found that people who are first subjected to difficult choices – what gift would you like to receive soon? – are quicker to pull their hand out of a basin of ice-cold water than people who are not. Here too: willpower does not seem to be inexhaustible.

Thus, research confirms that people who rely on their willpower to control their impulses will at some point run up against their own limits. People who have ever followed a diet are undoubtedly familiar with the principle of ego depletion. Changing eating habits formed over years by denying yourself all goodies demands constant self-control. Anyone who has followed such a diet can probably attest to the fact that his or her mood (certainly in the beginning) is not exactly improved by the experience. Research confirms this: dieters react more emotionally and impulsively than those who do not have to monitor their eating habits constantly. As a result, some people think eating salad makes them unhappy, while the feeling of uncontrollable emotions has more to do with the principle of exhausted willpower. People who stop smoking also have experience with this principle. Certainly at first, they don't seem able to concentrate or control their emotions. Not because cigarettes bring happiness or foster concentration, but because they are constantly balancing on the edge of ego depletion.

There are a number of methods for avoiding or reducing the effects of ego depletion. One is to apply an "if-then" strategy to various tasks. For every task you execute, you can reward yourself. In this way you create a good feeling between tasks, so that you start your second task with a more positive attitude. You can also introduce a brief pause between tasks that require self-control. Over time, you will feel for yourself how long this pause should be. It's also important to look after your physical well-being. If you're tired or hungry, you will reach the limits of your willpower more quickly. So do top up your energy reserves.

Those who wish to increase self-control in themselves, in the workplace or in society cannot ignore ego depletion. To understand it properly, it is important to note that the principle of ego depletion does not mean that you can't increase your self-control. Baumeister compared self-control with muscles: without training, we can't use them and will quickly reach the point of exhaustion. Too much training just before an important game has the same effect: you start tired and overtrained and will never deliver a peak performance. But a carefully constructed training program with small but regular exercises can indeed increase self-control.

Researchers at the University of New South Wales in Australia conducted a trial in which students were asked to use their weaker hand for daily tasks for two weeks. The students who were successful showed significantly more self-control after only two weeks when confronted with aggression. To switch over to the "other hand," people had to suppress their natural impulses. If they can do this in one specific area (in this case, by using their weaker hand), they are apparently able to suppress their natural reactions in other situations as well.

CONTROL YOURSELF CONSCIOUSLY

If you take these four principles into account, self-control is much more attainable than is often assumed. By restoring faith in delayed gratification, not undermining intrinsic motivation through reward systems, building in self-regulation through distraction, and respecting the limits of ego depletion, we gain more control over our own lives.

Everything starts with a proper understanding of how these four principles influence your self-control. But insight and understanding alone are not enough. We also have to translate these principles into practice and make them a reality. In order to take this step, we must rely on another tool of resilience: our consciousness. Self-control has a basis in the unconscious (think of the mechanisms of intrinsic motivation) as well as the consciousness (through self-regulation). Consciously engaging self-control is more than just deliberately trying to influence willpower; it is also about converting unconscious mechanisms into conscious strategies.

How you can learn to control yourself is also evident in the story of my client Sandrine, who had trouble with self-control. Sandrine felt strongly that she was being controlled by her impulses and that her negative ideas about work were constantly getting the upper hand. Together we looked for ways to better detect those impulses and replace them with a distracting thought. During moments of stress, for example, she would pay attention to her breathing, how the air was inhaled and exhaled through her nose. Of course this technique doesn't work for everyone – each person must discover what works best for him or her. In Sandrine's case, the principle of ego depletion was also crucial. She often exhausted herself before the day had even really started. Now she plans her most important tasks in the morning, when people have most mental energy, and ensures that distractions are kept to a minimum. In the afternoon, when her energy level is lower, she makes time for routine tasks such as answering e-mails or catching up with administration.

Why Archimedes ran naked through the streets

Consciously engaging your consciousness

. . . .

THE NARROW DOOR TO OUR CONSCIOUSNESS

Where were you this morning? After you stepped into the car or got on the train, before you arrived at the office ... Where were your thoughts then? Can you still remember what was going through your head in that hour or half hour? If you think hard, you might remember that crazy driver or the woman sitting next to you on the train who couldn't sit still. Maybe you spent some time worrying about your kids or an assignment you just can't seem to finish. But these concerns probably didn't take up the whole time. So where were you the rest of the time?

"Cogito, ergo sum," or "I think, therefore I am." Psychologists and philosophers have been grappling with the question of human consciousness for centuries. For a long time it was assumed that, as thinking beings, humans had no choice but to be self-conscious. The opposite of Descartes' famous slogan: "I am, therefore I think." Only with the advent of modern neurological research was this vision tempered and even completely demolished. Humans think, it is true, but certainly not all the time. Our consciousness is not something that automatically turns on whenever we open our eyes in the morning, but rather a mode that we can turn on and off.

The internationally renowned Dutch neuroscientist Bernard Baars compares consciousness to a theater in his groundbreaking Global Workspace Theory. In the theater of our consciousness, a spotlight shines on the podium. The illuminated area shows the parts of our consciousness. Actors that appear offer explanations or interact with each other. The public is not lit, and therefore not visible. Nor are the wings, where the director, writers, stage managers and prompters sit. They determine what the public gets to see, but they themselves are not visible.

Over the past 20 years, scientists have made some remarkable findings about the "theater of our consciousness." To start with, we can receive information not only consciously but also unconsciously. This may go against our ideas about consciousness, yet everyone has had experience with unconscious perception and processing. For example, when you get angry at a teenager because whatever you say to him seems to go in one ear and out the other. Or when you try to read a report while a nearby colleague is talking on the phone. We hear and see the information that comes to us, our senses are open, but it doesn't really get through.

The difference between "conscious consciousness" and "unconscious consciousness" is clearly visible in brain scans. When we are not paying attention to something, the information only enters as sensory experience and remains in that part of the brain where stimuli from our senses enter. Only when we take in information attentively does the input continue on to that part of the brain that can make connections and compare with the past, can contextualize things and make our decisions possible.

The phenomenon of "unconscious consciousness" explains why some things just don't seem to get through to our brains. But also why we can recite entire passages of Latin or even Korean (think: "Gangnam Style") texts without understanding a word.

Although the existence of this state of "unconscious consciousness" was only recently uncovered in Baars' research, there's no doubt that people dealt with it centuries ago. On the other hand, there is reason to believe that we have more to do with that half-brain-dead self today than we did before. The door to our conscious consciousness is narrow. Only one thing can actually pass through it at a time. Our brain is just physically incapable of consciously taking in several things at once. And this is precisely what we try to do on a grand scale today by multitasking. Yet however hard we try, we won't succeed in getting several thoughts and tasks through the door of our consciousness at once.

OUTINGS OF THE MIND

We live in an age of permanent distraction. We are surrounded by information that asks for – even demands – our attention. The mobile phone rings, our e-mail program lets us know we have new mail, social networks beg to be seen and everywhere we go, screens and sound installations inundate us with news and entertainment. Our mind resembles a loose cannon that is catapulted back and forth between all those attention magnets.

To escape all this input, our mind automatically slips into a state of unconscious consciousness. Matthew

Killingsworth and Daniel Gilbert, two psychologists at Harvard University who have studied the phenomenon of mind wandering, discovered that we're not really doing what we think we're doing at least 47 percent of the time. Even when we really apply ourselves to something, our mind is absent 30 percent of the time.

The idea that we're hovering around in the air somewhere half the time may seem overwhelming, but there are plenty of examples in everyday life. You walk up the stairs and enter a room. You know you were looking for something, but you no longer have the slightest idea what it was. You keep staring at the room in the hope of finding something that jogs your memory and leads you back to your original intent. It seems like instant dementia. Only when you get back downstairs does it pop into your head.

You are listening to a colleague's argument during a meeting, but by the time he asks you what you think, your thoughts are far away. You can only repeat his last few words. Embarrassed, you have to admit: "Sorry, I wasn't listening just now." You're reading a book at the swimming pool, but halfway through the second chapter you have to go back to the beginning because you no longer know what you just read. Someone asks you how the film was that you went to see at the movie theater yesterday, but you can't remember the title anymore. You meet a colleague on the street. You want to introduce him to your partner, but even though you see him every day, his name eludes you. How old is your son? "Six. No – eight." And your keys, where are they now? It's no longer the privilege of the absent-minded professor or the dippy hippy to be confronted with this sort of blackout.

The American neurologist Wendy Hasenkamp at Emo-
ry University investigated what precisely happens in our
brain when our mind wanders. She asked 14 people to meditate daily in an fMRI scanner. According to Hasenkamp,
meditation is highly sensitive to wandering minds. What's
more, the purpose of meditation is to teach us how to recognize more quickly the mind's propensity to check out. The
test subjects were all fervent meditation practitioners and
therefore trained "mind wanderers."

The participants were asked to push a button whenever
they noticed that their mind strayed from their meditation.
During a meditation of only 20 minutes, this happened on
average every 80 seconds. Bringing the mind back to meditation lasted on average a total of 12 seconds.

What happens in our brain when we are not there can
be compared to an airplane that flies on autopilot, according to Hasenkamp. We switch over to a "default mode." That
autopilot is in the medial prefrontal cortex, an area that is
associated with long-term memory, making associations,
processing emotions and the perception of time.

That precisely this area becomes active when we let our
minds run free suggests that mind wandering in itself is
not a waste of time. On the contrary, a wandering mind is a
mind that can make connections, put things in context and
process emotions. Killingsworth and Gilbert even describe
mind wandering as "a remarkable evolutionary achievement that allows humans to learn, reason and plan." In this
stressful society, in which we always seem to be hopping
from one "to do" to the other, it certainly can't hurt to give
our minds more freedom occasionally.

The problem with "mind wandering" is not that it happens but when it happens and how it affects us. In a meeting, right before a deadline, even behind the wheel of a car. It happens to our minds at inopportune times and embarrasses or even endangers us.

Another problem with these outings of the mind is that they disproportionately cause us to drift into negative feelings. This was one of the more disturbing findings of Killingsworth and Gilbert's research. Previous studies had already shown that unhappy people's thoughts strayed more frequently, but this was the first investigation that showed that the opposite was also true: participants in the study reported significantly more negative feelings when their minds were wandering than when they were concentrating.

All the old philosophical traditions advise people to fight unwanted thoughts and live as much as possible in the here and now, to be conscious of the moment. And now, thanks to science, we finally know why: a wandering mind is an unhappy mind.

It is no secret that the worse we feel, the less we pay attention. But the reverse is also true. The more we lose control of our thoughts, the worse we feel. Heartbreak is a good example. If our love life isn't going well, nothing seems to be going well. A broken relationship is very distracting and because we're so inattentive, we don't seem to be able to enjoy anything.

However, researchers distinguish between wandering stimulated by the environment and that provoked by emotional thoughts. The first form can be considered an activation of the archiving feature in our brain, as described by Killingsworth and Gilbert. By allowing your attention to wander briefly, you give your brain time to process and store information. You understand that this form of mind wandering is very useful. The second form is associated with sliding off into negative feelings. As contradictory as it may seem at first glance, this type of mind wandering also has its uses. I will return to this topic on (p. 97), in the section on conscious mind wandering.

THREE TECHNIQUES FOR
A MORE CONSCIOUS CONSCIOUSNESS

The modern individual's relationship with his or her wandering mind is ambivalent to say the least. On the one hand, we're irritated that we cannot keep our attention focused; on the other, we instinctively feel that our mind is over-exerted and needs to "float around out there for a while." The solution to both problems is contained in a single answer: by training the consciousness, we can learn to concentrate better – but also to relax better.

TECHNIQUE 1
Mindfulness

Mindfulness is currently very fashionable. Everywhere you look, you are advised to be more "mindful," whether it's about controlling your thoughts or tasting the food on your plate. Mindfulness is often seen as an attitude of "acceptance" in life, in which you try as much as possible to live in the moment.

What is often overlooked is that the state of acceptance is not the result of choosing to be more mindful in life, but of training through meditation. Mindfulness is in the first place a technique. John Kabat-Zinn, the father of modern mindfulness, even says that without training you will never become mindful. It's not a philosophy you can adhere to; it's a practice that needs to be exercised. You can read as many mindfulness books as you like, but unless you also start meditating, they won't help.

The reasons why mindfulness is so popular are not difficult to identify. It is one of the few techniques that is effective in battling chronic depression and anxiety disorders.

Even perfectly happy people can use mindfulness training in order to concentrate better, improve their performance and more consciously engage their consciousness. After all, mindfulness requires you to concentrate on the moment – for example, by consciously attending to your breath. This is a quintessential activity in which the mind starts to wander. People new to meditation often become frustrated because their thoughts are wandering the whole time. What they might not know is that that's the idea. The goal of attention meditation is to learn to recognize these outings of the mind and return to the original activity more quickly: focusing on the breath. By training regularly, those who practice mindfulness can also apply these techniques to everyday life and call their straying minds to attention more quickly.

The MBSR training (Mindfulness Based Stress Reduction) developed by John Kabat-Zinn has shown positive results in this area: this training reduces detectable symptoms of depression, anxiety and stress. Recently, even more striking results were found: one day of intensive mindfulness brought about changes in the genetic expression of certain molecules. Neuroscientists subjected participants in the United States, Spain and France to eight hours of mindfulness meditation and a control group to quiet, non-meditative activities. Prior to the experiment there was no difference in gene expression between the two groups; after eight hours, the difference was clear. The genes responsible for inflammation were less active in the meditating group. Future research will teach us how exercises in mindfulness and attention can be used to help reduce inflammation and pain.

On a physical as well as a mental level, the effects of mindfulness are overwhelming. The technique has also found its way into the business world. Successfully so. In his famous TED talk, mindfulness expert Andy Puddicombe said that "ten minutes of mindfulness per day" could make a world of difference for a company. This is now supported by research: after a brief meditation session, employees are better able to concentrate and are more productive. A number of apps have also been developed – by Puddicombe himself, among others – to offer meditation sessions custom-made for the modern employee (such as Buddhify, Headspace and Focus at Will). Many companies are taking steps to get their employees meditating, and in 2010, the Institute for Mindful Leadership was established in the United States, in which executives from General Mills, Cargill, BNP Paribas, Intel, Duke University and Procter & Gamble are active. Since then, the National Health Interview Survey (held every five years in the US) has kept a record of the percentage of employees who meditate. Their number has more than doubled since 2012.

TECHNIQUE 2

Thinking about thinking

"What are you thinking?" We are asked this question more often than we would like. Not because we don't want to share our thoughts, but because the question confronts us with the fact that we might not have had any thoughts at all. An important part of engaging more consciously with our consciousness is the creation of a metaconsciousness.

Most of the time our thoughts wander without us noticing. Only if the wandering is interrupted do we discover that our minds were elsewhere. Nonetheless, detecting our own train of thought is an important way to gain more control over our unconscious and conscious consciousness.

Researchers observed that you can increase your meta-consciousness by regularly asking yourself what you were thinking. How simple is that: at regular intervals or during moments of boredom (in the car during a traffic jam, waiting in line) actively ask yourself: "What was I just thinking?" It seems too easy to be true, but with that one question you challenge your brain to map your thought process so that you don't get lost in it, but instead are able to walk around in it with much more awareness.

TECHNIQUE 3

Conscious mind wandering

You can only increase consciousness through meditation and metaconsciousness on one condition: those who want to go through life more consciously have to reserve time for being unconscious. If our mind wanders 47 percent of the time, that is also because it needs that time. Perhaps even more so. By becoming aware of the fact that you are not consciously active for half of the day, you already take a load off your consciousness. All work and no play makes Jack a dull boy. There are only 24 hours in a day, and without a break you simply won't get very far.

Daydreaming has a bad reputation. Many people think it's a useless activity. They associate it with a loss of concentration and hence with loss of time. But daydreaming also has positive effects. Think, for example, of working through particular emotional experiences. By allowing our attention to stray to these negative thoughts, our brain convinces us of the need to cope with the situation actively. Of course you shouldn't wind up in a vicious circle of negative thoughts. Research shows that spontaneously arising worrisome thoughts have a negative effect on our mood and can even contribute to depression. But worrisome thoughts that we stimulate consciously seem to have a positive effect and encourage more rapid trauma processing. In other words, to stop worrying, we have to start worrying more consciously.

We experience another positive effect of daydreaming when our thoughts are distracted by trivial matters in our surroundings. During this type of mind wandering, new ideas and plans for the future are given a chance. It's also a great way to rest your mind after completing a task. In this way, mind wandering can counter the effects of ego depletion: you literally clear your head and recharge your batteries so that you can start a new task with a fresh dose of willpower.

The main advantage of this kind of thought wandering is that it stimulates creativity. You're preparing a presentation and have been looking for a good way to structure it for half an hour. Something still isn't quite right about the structure of your argument, but what? Your thoughts stray to a stimulating conversation you had yesterday evening with a good friend. Chances are, if you look back at your screen, you'll suddenly see where that slide fits in much better. In hindsight, it's probably no accident that Archimedes was in his bath when he shouted "Eureka!" and (according to contemporary sources) ran naked through the streets. Isaac Newton lay napping under a tree when one of the greatest discoveries of modern times literally fell on his head. Many people find it frustrating that they don't come up with their best ideas when they're looking for them, but a growing body of research shows that this is typical of original ideas: they only turn up when you're not looking for them.

As it turns out, then, a little boredom in the workplace does not make people brain-dead – it makes them more creative. According to researchers at the University of California, the best thing you can do after a brainstorming session or statement of a problem is let employees do something really boring for about 15 minutes. In many cases, the solution will simply turn up of its own accord. If you give your mind the chance to wander, your brain can make connections between things that, previously, you would never have thought were related.

These conclusions are particularly interesting, especially for creative businesses. We pay too much attention to the conscious part of our minds and too little to its unconscious movements. Wouldn't it be useful to give mind wandering a place at work instead of trying to banish it altogether? I think it would be helpful to organize an occasional session when everyone can let their mind wander, individually and collectively. This will certainly foster creativity. As an individual you can also use mind wandering to deal with difficulties. When you have to solve a complex problem, for example, it's better not to force yourself to come up with the right solution. Instead of staring at the problem, let it go. Seek appropriate distraction. The solution will probably arrive when you least expect it.

By better attuning our consciousness and unconscious to each other, we can exercise more self-control and better allocate our attention. An important part of this process is focusing concentrated attention on the things that are important to us. Focus is, after self-control and consciously engaging your consciousness, the third pillar of resilience that I would like to discuss.

How you really play "I'm going on a trip and I'm taking ..."

The importance of focus

. . . .

WHAT EPKE ZONDERLAND CAN TEACH US

An Olympic arena can be a madhouse. Of course you don't see this on television, where everything seems to be smoothly coordinated and disciplined athletes are neatly dressed in their sporting attire. But in fact it's a madhouse. The competition is murder, there's a lot of jealousy and just before the contest begins, chaos always reigns. And there, in the midst of all the madness, a young man wanders calmly on to the track with his headphones. As if he was taking a stroll in the park on a Sunday. He stops for a moment and stares at something in the distance, then walks on. Picks something up off the ground (or was that a stretching exercise?), turns his head in the other direction, and then runs deliberately towards the horizontal bar. A blond angel of a boy, lost in a world of chaos.

This is how Kasper Janssen, the sports doctor of the Dutch gymnastics team, described to me the preparations of Olympic gold winner and horizonal bar world champion Epke Zonderland. "He sees his opponents, but he is so focused that it's impossible for them to distract him." Later, I read in an interview exactly what Epke was doing at such moments. He concentrated by very calmly imagining how he would win. He visualized every part of the competition. His opponents were invisible to him. I was filled with admiration. What focus!

Not long after Epke's victory at the Olympic Games, I met someone who made his story even more remarkable. It happened when I wanted to take out an insurance policy. After some research, I found a firm that highlighted its client friendliness and personal approach. I sent an e-mail that was answered almost immediately by a woman I will call Anna. Within an hour, we had set an appointment for an initial consultation. A week later, Anna met me at her office, to explain why I should choose her firm and no other. In the hour I spent with her, Anna received three incoming calls (which she answered), three "urgent" e-mails (which she answered) and texted without stopping the whole time. Meanwhile, she explained in great detail the vision and operation of her firm and why I absolutely had to become their customer.

As I was leaving, she asked what I did for a living. I answered that as a psychologist, I helped businesses and people who wanted to increase their mental resilience and engagement. "Ah, then I'll probably come to see you soon," she said. "I have such a hard time concentrating." I told her I could believe it and gave her my card. "If I have five minutes to spare," she laughed, typing a number into her smartphone with her thumb while opening the door. With her telephone already clamped to her ear, she waved goodbye. I never saw her again, nor she me.

Anna said everything that was expected of an insurance agent; her arguments were good. But I didn't feel safe with her. Anna lacked one very important quality: attention.

Even though what she said was believable, I didn't feel like she took me seriously because she was busy with other things and other people the entire time.

I also don't know what motivated her to act this way. Perhaps she wanted to make a good impression by showing how much work she had, how many contracts she serviced and how quickly she responded to everyone. And I have to admit that in the beginning I was charmed by how quickly she had responded to my first e-mail. Unfortunately, my initial appreciation melted like snow in the sun after our conversation.

THE ATTENTION ECONOMY

With Epke on one side and Anna on the other, it is immediately obvious why focus is so important and why it's growing in importance daily. We are all intelligent today. Or almost. The so-called Flynn effect shows that our IQ has risen three points every decade since World War II. So we're smarter than our grandparents. Another study, however, led by Michael Woodley of Umea University in Sweden, reveals that our reaction time is slower than it was a century ago. Although it's difficult to say exactly what factors cause this delayed reaction time, I am convinced that focus (or lack thereof) plays an important role.

How well do we concentrate? If we're honest, we might not be much better than Anna. Many of us have the feeling that we're in constant contact with everyone. While we're phoning, we're looking at our e-mail; if we're catching up with friends at a bar, we're looking at social media at the same time to see what other friends are doing and also checking our e-mail from work. Because we might get one of those oh-so-important messages that has to be answered within the hour. Why do we do it? Out of fear that we'll miss all kinds of important things – fear of missing out – is the first possibility. But also because we're addicted to the idea that we're indispensable. Moreover, we're afraid of the consequences of social exclusion. Mattering and being recognized is vital. The telephone can never be turned off during a meeting or a lecture, because "what if that one client or colleague calls?" Even in the toilet and the bedroom, the technology comes with us. Today we want the news and the radio and the newspaper and articles on the Internet all day long, because if we don't keep up, we no longer count.

Never have we been so connected, never have we paid so little attention. And this has consequences, not least for our memory. Try answering the following question: What were the most important news items of the past year? You might remember a few things that made a lasting impression, but for the rest you probably had to dig deep. We can make it more difficult by asking: What were the most important news items of five years ago? Most people will have no idea. Then, for a lesson in humility, visit your (grand) parents and ask them what the most important news items were 50 years ago. Chances are that they can still give you a detailed answer to your question.

Our memory has become a sieve. Most people are aware of this. Researchers from various disciplines have spent years trying to figure out why. Why do we have such a hard time remembering things today? Psychologists at the University of Columbia point an accusing finger in the direction of the Internet, which we intuitively think of as a kind of back-up memory, so that we no longer bother to remember things ourselves. Other studies point to changes in our diet and sleep patterns to explain the deterioration of our memory, but clearly something else is involved as well. Perhaps the most important revolution the new century has brought with it is the technological revolution. And its biggest victim is our attention.

The internationally renowned sociologist and psychologist Herbert Simon predicted this back in 1971: "In an information-rich world, the wealth of information means a dearth of something else: a scarcity of whatever it is that information consumes. What information consumes is rather obvious: it consumes the attention of its recipients. Hence a wealth of information creates a poverty of attention and a need to allocate that attention efficiently among the overabundance of information sources that might consume it."

Forty years later, this principle formed the basis for the theory of the "attention economy," which was elaborated by business strategists Thomas Davenport and Michael Goldhaber, among others. In their analysis, attention is on the verge of replacing money as the most important economic medium of exchange because it is rarer and hence more valuable today. To put it simply: those who can attract attention fastest get the power, regardless of the product. In advertising, journalism, the music industry and cyberspace, this is already a reality, and is at the root of the current furore around "fake news."

The conclusion is clear. Attention is what matters, on an individual as well as on a societal level. Without attention, there can be no self-control or grit. In addition, attention is the basic precondition of flow. Only with attention can we be successful and happy. No focus, no profit.

WHAT FOCUS REALLY IS

The problem with focus is this. We all know that we want to be able to focus more and better, but actually we don't know what focus really is. In neuroscience, directing attention is of one of the brain's three executive functions, all of which pass through the prefrontal cortex. The other two are solving tasks and memory. All of these functions are linked.

In neuroscientist Bernard Baars' metaphor for consciousness, focus is the place on the stage where we aim the spotlight. To be able to direct our attention, a certain degree of control over our consciousness is required. Focus is the state of concentrated attention that ensures that we look only at the illuminated area.

Daniel Goleman, author of the bestseller *Emotional Intelligence*, which has been translated into more than 40 languages, distinguishes three types of focus in his recent book, *Focus*: an inward focus, a focus on others, and an outward focus. According to Goleman, all three kinds are needed to make the difference between a "loser" and a "leader."

He describes inward-looking or inner focus as the attention someone pays to his or her own intuition, norms and values. In Baars' theater metaphor: the people behind the scenes. Focus on others is the attention we devote to the people around us – the public, as it were. This is the sort of attention that the insurance agent Anna expended so lavishly that she ended up shortchanging everyone (especially her physical conversation partner at the time). Outward-looking or outer focus is the attention we give to the greater whole: the theater.

But in addition to the three forms of focus Goleman describes, there is a very sober, manageable kind of focus we use in our daily lives. Let's call this type of focus "concentrated attention," the type that led Epke to victory. All these forms of attention are inseparable from one another. We will begin with the most tangible form: concentrated attention. How can we improve it?

THE MAGIC NUMBER SEVEN (PLUS OR MINUS TWO)

First, let's look at how our potential for concentrated attention develops naturally. This can easily be compared to the way a muscle evolves. Its strength is to some extent genetically determined, but immediately after birth we can barely use our muscles. Through trial and error, we become stronger, learn how to deploy our strength and use it efficiently.

The same is true for concentrated attention. In a certain sense, it's in our genes, but we have to exercise this talent. A baby only succeeds in consciously directing its attention after a couple of months. Through extensive training, we can succeed in concentrating longer. A one-year-old has difficulty concentrating on something for a minute; toddlers can usually focus for up to ten minutes. After that, the systematic growth of our attention span does not increase dramatically. In adults, the scope for concentrated attention is between 10 and 40 minutes.

Although comparative studies are difficult, a growing number of researchers claim that our attention span has decreased dramatically in recent decades. Just as your muscles weaken when you stop exercising, your attention also deteriorates if you don't use it. It's also also true that if you make a concerted effort to train and exercise your focus, you can strengthen it considerably.

But watch out! Just as a muscle can be overstressed and exhausted, you can also strain your focus. One of the most frequently cited studies in cognitive psychology is a text from 1956 by George Miller, often known as the father of cognitive psychology. The title is evocative: "The magical number seven, plus or minus two: some limits on our capacity for processing information." In the paper, Miller explains how our working memory can always retain approximately seven things on different planes. How this theory, also known as "Miller's Law", works is easy to explain using a game I used to play as a child: "I'm going on a trip and I'm taking…"

For those who aren't familiar with it, the game is played as follows. You sit in a circle and each player chooses something to help finish the sentence. The first takes a toothbrush on the trip, for example, the second a pair of underpants, the third a suitcase, and so on. The difficulty is that each child must repeat all the things that went before. At the start it's usually pretty easy, but there's always a point when most children can't remember all the preceding items. That moment – let's call it the sum test – is usually around number seven.

According to Miller's Law, our working memory can't keep track of more than around seven (in the best case nine, in the worst case five) successive information units at a time. Therefore, wine tasters can't distinguish more than seven glasses of wine at a time; you you can't differentiate more than seven fragments of music in one sitting; advertising panels never mention more than seven things; and you can remember about seven random numbers at once.

When I was young, we didn't like playing this game. There were two girls who could keep adding things to the trip without end. This was very frustrating for the other children, who had to wait until they finished their packing frenzy. Even the group leaders couldn't keep up. I always asked myself how they did it. Thanks to Miller's Law, I finally understood after all those years. The way to elude the rule of seven is to group separate tasks into clusters. The 'magic number seven' can always be subdivided into four clusters and three individual things. By putting information units together in a linked series, you can increase your attention span. However, you can only work up to four, and after that add only three new units. Until you make four new clusters and three new units. This is how the girls were able to increase their attention span – at least for a while.

FINDING YOUR FOCUS

There is little doubt that there's a limit to the extent to which we can deploy our focused attention. Not only in time, but also in number. But there are ways to increase our attention span and generally improve our focus. The way our consciousness works, however, often makes the task more complicated than we'd hoped.

"Think! Think! Think!" I sometimes hear myself say. And then I know it's a lost cause. It means that I'm concentrating too hard on what I'm doing, so that I forget how to do it. That's the annoying thing about focus: you don't achieve it just by trying harder. With self-control alone you won't get there.

I have already discussed the first and most important strategy for living more attentively and it has to do with the way we interact with our consciousness. This means taking time to be inattentive. To stay with the theater metaphor: we simply cannot stand on the stage day and night; the spotlight has to be turned off now and then. It sounds so obvious, but I notice daily how difficult people find it to put this basic rule into practice.

A second, equally obvious strategy is just as difficult to put into practice: setting priorities. Many people feel that they're not leading their own lives, but that their lives are being directed from outside. And in many cases it's true. Too often we allow ourselves to be swept along by the issues of the day. Yet again we're consumed by people, things, feelings and events that overcome us to the point that we lose sight of the bigger picture.

Being more attentive begins with setting goals and priorities. Not only in the short term (first I want to finish this task, and then if I still have time, I'll start on the next one), but also in the long term. The question "What do I actually want to get out of my life?" may seem undefined, and to some even useless, but it has a huge impact on our daily lives. Just imagine discovering that you felt bad all this time because you weren't living according to your own priorities. If freedom is your most important motivation, perhaps it's a good idea to structure your work situation accordingly. The other way around is much more difficult. If you live for your children, you'll probably want to see them more often. If you like being with people, you might not want to live out in the country. And so on. Only by paying attention to our priorities can we attend to those things that are important to us and thus find our focus.

RETAINING YOUR FOCUS

Finding focus is one part of the story; the other is retaining your focus. We live in an age of permanent distraction and "infobesity." The trick is to not let ourselves be swept along by the wave of information, but to continue to set our own course. This does not mean that you have to cut off all technology and information streams – this is often impossible – but you do have to develop a strategy that makes it possible to manage the avalanche of information.

Fortunately, we as humans have an exceptional ability to adjust our environment according to our wishes. Granted, our problems with attention are largely context-related. We live in busy times. But that doesn't have to stop us from taking responsibility for ourselves. With small, practical interventions in your daily life, you can help your brain turn the spotlight on and point it at what is important. Just like self-control and consciously engaging your consciousness, focus can also be trained.

We've only just discovered this. For a long time, scientists assumed that the ability to find and retain attention was largely fixed in our working memory, because it is so strongly anchored in the prefrontal cortex. For this reason, it was long assumed that only the symptoms of typical attention disorders such as ADHD could be treated. Professor Torkel Klingberg of the Karolinska Institute in Sweden was one of the first to challenge this. In 2002, this neuroscientist subjected children with attention problems to a computerized training scheme for the working memory. They were also given daily cognitive tasks of approximately half an hour long for five weeks. The training (afterwards this was deemed crucial to the result) was set up so that the degree of difficulty increased as the children became better at the exercises.

The results of the study were astonishing. After the training was completed, the children showed considerable improvement in their working memory, a decrease in attention problems and hyperactivity, and an increase in their reasoning and problem-solving skills. These effects were still evident three and even five months later.

Later, similar results were observed among adults who had suffered a stroke. There was an increase in working memory as well as an improvement in their ability to pay attention. Klingberg and his colleagues have shown in the meantime how this effect takes shape in the brain. Using fMRI analyses, they observed that brain activity in the prefrontal cortex, among other places, increased considerably after targeted training. The density of specific cortical dopamine receptors also increased. This last finding underscores the plasticity of our brain, even after only 14 hours of training spread over five weeks.

This kind of training research has been frequently copied and repeated. Brain training is breaking through on a large scale, not only in the treatment of ADHD, but also in the battle against age-related dementia and other attention disorders. At Erasmus University in Rotterdam, we conducted several studies to test the effectiveness of working memory training among people with a depressive disorder, an anxiety disorder or an addiction. The idea is that symptoms of these disorders are in part caused by a faulty working memory. The research, led by Sabine Wanmaker, showed that it it's difficult to develop a training program that not only strengthens the working memory, but also reduces specific symptoms.

Working memory training programs are increasingly finding their way into the workplace, given that they have a considerable effect on people's attention span. We have also tested employees in several companies on their cognitive fitness. Depending on their specific results, they are given extra training for several weeks. The results are highly encouraging: employees reported that they were more alert, could hold their attention longer during meetings and thus got more out of them. The training also seemed to have an effect on the experience of stress: employees gained greater control over their thoughts, so probably spent less time worrying.

Using heightened consciousness to take attention and self-control in hand is the springboard to resilience. But with mental and cognitive resilience alone, we won't get there. Not yet. The leverage that is missing – the fourth and final mainspring of resilience – is also the glue that holds the other cogs together. It is emotional leverage – optimism. Optimism doesn't appear at the start of this story, but at the end and it also forms the driving force in the upward spiral.

The explanation for everything

The power of optimism

· ·

THE CANCER QUINTET

Cees Huijing pours himself a gin and tonic. I'm immediately struck with how boyish this creative man in his seventies looks. Cees is full of fascinating stories. About how he skated 200 km over natural ice during the last traditional Dutch Elfstedentocht (Eleven Cities Tour) how he won a sailing regatta and several prestigious golf matches. But also how he started his own advertising agency at the age of 30 and became a successful businessman.

But we talk mostly about "after," about the period after the successes. When Cees left his advertising agency to his two sons five years ago, he became seriously ill. Bladder cancer was the diagnosis. After a very complex operation, Cees had a stroke that paralyzed his entire left side. He lost around 40 pounds but kept at it for five months in the hospital, fighting to free his left side from paralysis. He could rely on the unceasing support of his loving wife, assisted by one son, who would arrive each morning at the hospital with freshly pressed juices, and by his other son, who smuggled in alcohol-free beers in the evening.

Cees won the battle. Determined that cancer wouldn't get the better of him, he took up his old hobbies again – including golf. And won another match. One year later the cancer was back. This time too, he recovered. After that the illness came back a third time and doctors declared his situation "hopeless."

A couple of months after the third diagnosis, Cees was back on the golf course. Doctors call him a medical miracle, but Cees just wants to live. And how glad he is that he still can. Out of gratitude for his own life, Cees now devotes himself to raising funds for cancer research, together with his so-called "cancer quintet." After his illness, Cees and four other affluent and powerful friends who had also survived cancer made a pact that they would stimulate research into the early diagnosis of cancer. The five of them have raised millions for research.

Some people would say that Cees is "in denial" about the seriousness of his condition. Others might call him a desperate optimist, but for me, Cees is the best example of someone who has learned to grow through adversity. He is very consciously occupied with his psyche ("when I used to have business stress, I cycled it off; it doesn't make sense to spend long nights worrying"), with his fellow humans ("my wife is my queen") and his resilience ("I keep physically fit, but a fit brain is only needed for getting work done"). Cees is a true optimist.

INNATE OPTIMISM

Optimism can border on madness. Some people say optimism of any kind is a form of self-deception or even hallucination. There is something to be said for this view. The only thing we know for certain about our future is that it will come to an end. The chance that we will experience misfortune in our lives is somewhere around 100 percent. Aren't we, with all we know today about the climate, the economy and world peace, particularly naive to keep believing in the future? Is there a Candide hidden in every one of us, who, just like the character in Voltaire's eponymous masterpiece, continues to believe in a sort of justness to his destiny, even in the most piteous circumstances?

Study after study, survey after survey confirms: as human beings we are destined to keep believing, unceasingly, indefatigably, in the future. Because of this we consistently underestimate the risks we run of traffic accidents and illness, but seriously overestimate our chances in a job interview or with a member of the opposite sex. Millions of people buy a lottery ticket every week because they're convinced of their luck. Even in the deepest economic crisis, we believe that things will get better soon, and even when all the doctors tell us it's not going well, we continue to hope for a miracle. The answer is yes, we are incorrigible optimists and no, we can't do anything about it.

Optimism, as evolutionary biologists have discovered, is a crucial element of our survival instinct. In particular, it forms a counterweight to our huge intelligence. Thanks to our ingenious human brain, we can estimate situations more accurately than other animal species, but with realism alone we wouldn't have made it very far. Would we still run away from a tiger if we always had to calculate how much faster he can run than us? Would we eat anything at all if we constantly had to stop and think about the origin of our food and its possible negative effects?

Knowledge, without the tempering effect of optimism, has an overwhelmingly paralyzing effect on people. In this sense, optimism is not the opposite of intelligence, but the counterweight that holds it up. Optimism without knowledge is fatal. Knowledge without optimism is just as deadly. For the survival of our species, we need both.

Because optimism is so deeply ingrained in our genes, it has often been used over the centuries by people who want to get things done by other people. Politicians and advertisers make liberal use of it. American election campaigns are a well-known example: slogans with a clear (though not necessarily realistic) future promise like "Make America Great Again" (Trump 2016) and "Yes We Can" (Obama 2008) invariably win against campaigns that focus on the here and now. In fact, you could say that the entire existence of the United States is predicated on that idea, but even in Europe the concept is catching on. You don't win elections by emphasizing how well things are going, but by promising change. And in the advertising world, this attitude is avidly manipulated. Even critical consumers like to believe that they will be healthy if they eat a certain kind of yogurt, that their children will be overjoyed with this type of toy, that they will be successful if they drive this car, that their house will only really be beautiful with this brand of kitchen.

LEARNED OPTIMISM

Optimism sells and optimism pays. Research shows that optimists live longer, have a better chance of survival when confronted with illness and after operations, that they are less subject to dementia and other symptoms of aging, that they are more successful and happier, and that they also draw out these qualities among those around them.

The question that has long occupied philosophers and

scientists is: Why? It was psychology that finally provided a conclusive answer. Since the 1970s, new studies have appeared every year showing that optimism is not just a congenital character trait. Optimism is also an attitude. That is to say, one person may have been born more optimistic than another, but you can also choose to be more optimistic in life.

We now know that you can learn and train optimism. And because optimism has such a positive effect on so many levels, it has given rise to a real hype. Positive psychology is inundating the world with handbooks and recipes for happiness. The "makeable" human being, who makes his or her own choices and determines the course of his or her own life, is now also responsible for his or her own happiness.

SMILE OR DIE

Optimism has become a choice, and according to some even an obligation that we as humans must live up to. Sometimes it goes in the wrong direction. "Smile or die" is how the American journalist Barbara Ehrenreich described the current optimism hype. When she was diagnosed with cancer, she was mainly surprised by the reactions she received. Even before she had time to process the news, she was told that she "would come out of it stronger" and that cancer would bring her closer to pure happiness. The suggestion that she should be thankful for the illness – and that overcoming it was mostly a matter of positive thinking – bothered her so much that she wrote a book about it: *Smile or Die: How Positive Thinking Fooled America and the World*. In it, she rejects the idea that optimism is a sort of magic cure that is available to everyone, notes that allowing negative feelings is increasingly seen as some kind of stupid, asocial choice, and that failure is primarily a question of not having enough faith. The most extreme example is the ultra-popular book *The Secret*, in which Rhonda Byrne states that you can influence the universe to give you everything you want if you only think positively enough.

I'm not a big fan of the cult of the positive, in which everything always has to be "happy-happy." But I am convinced that better insight into the way optimism works can make a big difference in someone's life. You don't have to be an optimist to believe that. Research confirms it.

THE UR-INSTICT

How does optimism work? Given that optimism is one of humankind's basic motivations, it is not surprising that it is anchored in one of our oldest brain structures, the amygdala, better known as our fear center. Here lies the origin of the human "fight-or-flight" instinct, the modern variant of which is stress. Optimism, as neurological research has shown, shows itself in the brain primarily through the absence of stress. This does indeed seem to correspond to experience. People who have confidence in the future are less likely to get wound up if something threatens to go wrong. And conversely, anxious people worry more, even if nothing is apparently wrong. Although the research does not yet reveal which is the chicken and which is the egg – are you less bothered by stress because you're an optimist, or are you optimistic because you're less bothered by stress? – the link between the two is clear.

In addition to being the location for stress, the amygdala is also the place where emotions are linked to events. Thus, for our emotional lives, it is a very important part of the brain. That too corresponds to what our senses tell us: optimism is linked to happiness, just as depression is linked to pessimism, although it's not entirely clear in which direction the causal link goes. Nevertheless, much becomes clear if we look deeper into how optimism is anchored in our brain. We know, for example, that optimism has a lot to do with linking an emotion to an event. In part this is something that happens automatically, but at the same time, we can influence it more than we think. How we look back at the events in our lives has a lot to do with what in psychological research is known as the "explanatory style": the way in which we explain things.

EXPLANATORY STYLES

Explanatory styles can differ on three levels. These can be summed up as (1) who, (2) where and (3) when. The "who" style is about who caused the event. Pessimists are more inclined to look to themselves when seeking the cause of a negative event. If you stumble, you can berate yourself for being so clumsy, or get angry with the people who paved the street for not doing their job properly. Conversely, pessimists don't take credit for positive things that they actually did. If a pessimistic salesman sees his turnover increase by 10 percent, for example, he will attribute it to the fact that the economy is on the mend and people are therefore spending more money. He forgets all the hard work he invested in finding new customers.

The "where" style has to do with how you assess the magnitude of an event. Optimists see the consequences of their mistakes as fairly specific, while pessimists generalize them immediately. At times it seems as if all the red lights are waiting just for you, while you could just as easily have encountered green lights. After doing poorly on an exam, an optimistic student will think that at least she did well on four other exams and that the final results will probably be okay; a pessimistic colleague immediately thinks she will have to do the school year over.

Finally, the "when" style is the strongest component in distinguishing between an optimistic and a pessimistic explanatory style. Pessimists are usually convinced that everything that goes wrong, always goes wrong and always will go wrong, while optimists see negative experiences as chance occurrences from which they also can learn something. Take, for example, a major reorganization at work. Two colleagues have to change departments. The pessimist will blame himself because his recent performance hasn't been good enough. Therefore, he's now being shunted off to an inferior position. And there is nothing he can do to change it. His chance at a brilliant career is over. The optimist, by contrast, will see the situation as a challenge and make an effort to seize whatever opportunities arise. It might be less enjoyable for a while and mean a lot of extra hard work, he reasons, but maybe someday a position will open up in the department where he really wants to be. Optimists also tend to play a positive role in the smooth completion of a reorganization.

The style in which you explain the events in your life is not genetically determined; rather, it belongs to the learned part of optimism. Education and early life experiences have a profound influence on it. If you're immersed in a pessimistic atmosphere as a child and your parents emphasize that "you had best be careful, because in life you have to be prepared for the worst," it's unlikely that you will have an optimistic attitude towards life. Although explanatory styles can be tenaciously rooted, you can still change them later in life. You can exercise control over them – or at least you can if you're prepared to take on that responsibility.

THE ANSWER TO STRESS

Neurological research tells us that optimism has to do with the emotional interpretation of events. A second conclusion we can draw is that optimism in the brain is the opposite of stress. In reality, stress is the modern articulation of our ur-instinct to "fight" or "flee" when danger pops up. In prehistoric times, if you came across a lion you had to decide in a fraction of a second: either attack or run away as fast as possible. The choice between fight and flight happened instinctively, without thinking. Because in such situations, if you carefully weigh the pros and cons of each scenario, the lion will already have devoured you.

For most modern challenges, these physical reactions no longer make sense. However, our bodies still produce the stress hormones that in prehistoric times ensured that you fought or fled. Because these hormones are no longer ventilated, they continue to circulate in the body. This creates stress. This kind of stress isn't necessarily bad. The way you deal with it determines whether the stress will have a positive or a negative effect.

Here, too, we see a notable difference between optimists and pessimists. If we look at their "coping style," the way in which they handle stress, the two groups are diametrically opposed to one another. As a rule, pessimists employ a "passive coping" strategy. They tend to avoid challenges, evade problems, stick their heads in the sand and wait far too long before they seek help. Optimists are active processors. They seek out challenges, confront their problems directly, call on resources for help when necessary and try to find solutions.

If you're paying attention, you'll recognize the difference between the "fleers" and the "fighters" of prehistoric times. Pessimists tend to flee. If a lion crosses your path, fleeing is a good reaction. Unfortunately, this kind of flight behavior makes little sense in terms of most 21st-century challenges. You can run away from a lion if you run far enough; sooner or later you'll manage to shake him. But how do you run away from a deadline, an unpaid bill or a boring colleague? Modern problems have the tendency to follow their victims around, so fleeing in our society primarily means that we remain under constant stress.

Although "fighting or fleeing" has mostly to do with instinct, it does have a learned component. You can learn not to avoid challenges and this gets easier with every victory. But the opposite is also true: a negative experience can cause you to flee further and further away. A conflict at work can cause you to avoid particular places or colleagues, which generates extra stress. This stress makes you even more inclined to hide, until you have become a shadow of yourself and associate work only with stress. Instead, you could analyze the conflict and determine exactly what went wrong. You could then think up a solution, eventually confront your colleague, and hope for a solution to the problem. This has the effect of relieving stress and will help you to face conflicts in the future.

Another lesson we can learn from the research on negative stress and optimism is that the two are at opposite ends of the same scale. That is to say, they are in equilibrium: if optimism goes down, negative stress goes up, and if negative stress goes down, optimism goes up. This means we can also encourage optimism by reducing our stress level.

This explains why meditation training, sports and recreational pastimes really do make people happier. They reduce stress, which means optimism and therefore emotional well-being increase.

HOW MARTIN SELIGMAN ENGENDERED CHANGE

There is, in other words, reason to be optimistic about optimism. By paying attention to the way we explain events and making minor adjustments to it, by actively responding to challenges and reducing our stress level, we can change a great deal about our attitude and in this way increase our feeling of happiness. But there is more.

As I mentioned earlier, an entire industry has sprung up around optimism. All too often, it is limited to superficial analyses and rosy advice packaged in catchy slogans. But not with Martin Seligman, who is rightly called the "father of positive psychology." Seligman was not only the founder of positive psychology, but remains the undisputed king of this field of research. Even today he is the only one to have developed a truly workable model founded on scientific principles that suddenly makes optimism tangible.

Interestingly, Seligman did not start his scientific career on the positive side of the scale, but on the negative: with learned helplessness. In the 1960s, he conducted tests that showed that animals that do not get a chance to improve their situation (in this case, to avoid electrical shocks) over time become depressed and sick and lose their ability to learn. With people, too, "learned helplessness" also leads to psychological disorders such as depression.

Seligman's research was groundbreaking because it debunked the theory, current at the time, that we automatically adjust our behavior to our experiences. Before his study, people assumed that everything you do, think and feel is a behavior and that these behaviors can be described on the basis of external factors. Seligman's tests demonstrated for the first time the importance of mental processes in explaining human behavior. The study catapulted the young Seligman to the top of the new field of psychological science, where he still is after 50 years. It's not for nothing that he is considered one of the most important psychologists of the 20th century.

Just over 20 years ago, Martin Seligman changed his field of research from helplessness to human inventiveness and was thus at the dawn, together with flow expert Mihaly Csikszentmihalyi, of "positive psychology." In this brand-new scientific branch, attention is focused on everything that traditional psychology leaves out. Since then, Seligman has pursued the learning of inventiveness that increases people's happiness. In a word: optimism.

In 2011, after years of research, Seligman published his book *Flourish*, in which he presents the PERMA model for how to become happier. PERMA is an acronym that stands for five essential components of happiness that you as a human being can influence. P stands for positive emotion, E for engagement, R for relationships, M for meaning and A for achievement.

Positive emotion is probably the most obvious element of happiness, but also the most difficult to change. Positive emotions are, however, absolutely necessary to making more of our lives. Psychologist Barbara Fredrickson places the importance of emotional experiences at the top of her "broaden-and-build" approach to optimism. According to her, more happiness is in the first place a question of better balance in our emotional lives. For every negative emotion, we need three positive ones. Going in search of people and things that make you feel good is thus also the first step to repairing a negative mood.

We addressed engagement earlier when we discussed its relationship to flow. Apart from being more conscious of how we engage our consciousness (and especially by including more rest) and increasing our focus, we can also reach this state by starting every task with a more positive attitude. It is an investment that pays off quickly, as research shows, because flow does indeed make you happier.

Only lately have relationships been accorded more value by happiness researchers. Until recently, research was primarily directed at two levels: the level of objective experiences and the level of mental processes in every person. Happiness was considered the result of positive experiences, and also seen as the result of intrinsically positive emotions. Both neurological and psychological research point more and more in the direction of belonging as a key concept of happiness. The idea that happy people have more relationships is increasingly being turned around to mean that people with more relationships are happier.

Finding meaning in life has largely to do with the priorities that we as humans set, and is closely related to that which intrinsically motivates us. In this area, we as humans have deviated considerably from our instincts, as Seligman also affirms. The issues of the day govern not only our behavior, but also our thoughts. According to *Golden Circle* author Simon Sinek, the most important question in life is not what we do, but why we do it. We find the same position in Goleman's assertion that focus on the greater whole forms the basis of all attention.

The relationship between achievement and happiness is hotly debated by scientists. Although it goes against the grain, most researchers now agree that success does not make us happy, but happiness makes us successful. Nonetheless, Seligman adheres closely to the idea that achievement contributes to our happiness, but mainly in relation to our explanatory style. Only when we recognize our successes as our own will our feeling of happiness increase.

SLOPTIMISM

In scientific and in popular literature, the optimism hype is still far from receding. On the eve of the post-pharmaceutical age, more and more people are looking for ways to improve their quality of life through small adjustments and new ways of thinking. But the current interest in optimism also has its dangers.

The most obvious problem with optimism is the possibility that it will slide into irrealism. Those who are too optimistic are subject to pride, which as we all know leads to a fall. This phenomenon is especially familiar in medical science. The "optimistic bias" can lead to patients stopping their medication, or not believing their doctors when they bring bad news, or to the terminally ill cherishing false hope.

A second problem with optimism is that it can lead to "sloptimism," in which people become exceedingly sloppy because they assume that everything will turn out all right in the end. In this sense, optimism can be the opposite of perfectionism.

A third pitfall of optimism is related to this, and is about our relationship with stress. In general, we look for ways to reduce stress, but there are plenty of scenarios in which stress can save our lives – even today. As I said before, a certain degree of stress can have a positive impact. Stress makes us more alert and prepares us for physical or mental performance. Too much optimism in this sense can even be life-threatening.

People and companies that want to work on optimism would do well to keep these possible problems in mind, so that the balance doesn't tip too far in the other direction. For the rest, I do not think there is any reason to be pessimistic about optimism. For the most part, it remains a safe and promising strategy.

PART III

FOUR WAYS TO ARRIVE AT A BETTER BRAIN STRATEGY

Here I would like to be able to tell you that all of the above is a matter of daily practice for me. That I myself am a boundless optimist who has no trouble achieving flow through focus, who only allows her thoughts to wander when appropriate, and who never loses it with a bag of chips or in an online clothing store. That all the knowledge I've built up over the years about how to better your mind has automatically made me more resilient, happier, and more successful. And that as a result, you can become all these things just by reading this book.

But just as you don't become physically fitter by reading books about eating properly or become an excellent dancer by browsing through an encyclopedia of modern dance, it doesn't work like that with our minds either. To profit from all that knowledge, you have to put it into practice. You have to start somewhere and keep training when things get tough and continue until you no longer have to make an effort at all. I readily admit that I've never reached this last phase. I too have to decide each and every day to give my life direction, take responsibility for my own thoughts and invest in my own mind.

I realize, in other words, that the decision to invest in your mind is not an easy one. Not only for individuals, but perhaps even more so for policymakers, for people in business or education. It is still a relatively expensive and unknown investment. This is why there is still resistance to working out a definite brain strategy. Although, as I mentioned earlier, it is a risk-free investment, many are still waiting for a sign. To see what others do first and only then follow if needed.

While it's understandable, this doubt about responding to the current brain crisis is in my opinion unjustified. Today we know so much about our minds. With only 20 years of research, positive psychology may be the baby of the behavioral sciences, but it has already yielded impressive insights. Since the Decade of the Brain (1990s), neuroscience has also taught us a great deal about how we can lead a more successful, happier, more engaged life. Even better news is that scientists and internationally renowned authors ensure that knowledge of what it is that empowers our brain does not remain hidden away in laboratories and university libraries. On the contrary, few scientific fields enjoy as much public interest as positive psychology and neurology.

In the corporate world, you see a light go on here and there when a company actively seeks to collaborate with psychologists to cash in on mental capital. For the time being, however, we have to look at these far-sighted businesses as the first swallows of spring – they're a good sign, but their presence doesn't mean it's summer yet.

It also seems to me no coincidence that the people we consider the pioneers of mental capital started their investment primarily out of necessity. In many cases, the "law of the stimulative arrears," which I discussed in part I, played a key role. A negative experience nearly always served as the basis for their decision to actively invest in resilience. A burnout suddenly makes the search for resilience very urgent. A sudden increase in absenteeism or loss of personnel makes companies reach for mental training programs.

Better late than never, of course, and as we know the greatest success stories emerge from crises. But in itself, this is a missed opportunity. If coaching and training can make such a difference for people who, in terms of mental capital, are temporarily lower than zero, what effect might it have on people who still have some startup capital?

With the right investments, leaders and policymakers can make a big difference, certainly in sectors that are largely dependent on the brain power of their employees as the key means of production. Without a brain strategy, companies and institutions that rely on the creativity of their employees will quickly feel the effects of the brain crisis. By extension, all companies involved with innovation will benefit from a sound brain strategy. The government itself belongs by definition to the brain sector, given that it is charged with setting out and elaborating policy for society.

One of the sectors in which scientific insights seem to trickle down slowly is education. Although education is clearly experiencing the effects of the brain crisis, investments remain limited. But it is precisely in education that such an investment is crucial, not only for the education sector itself, but for the future of our society in general.

Thanks to scientific research, we now have the chance to educate a generation that is stronger and more resilient than all those that have gone before. The alternative is less attractive. If we don't use our knowledge on bettering minds in education, the following generation may be the least resilient ever. Research has also shown that the "digital generation," which has grown up surrounded by and in part raised by technology, is unfortunately less able to cope with the challenges of the 21st century. The side effects on the children and youth of today are even clearer than they were for the "analog generation": behavioral problems, decreased psychological well-being, loss of ability to think critically, decreased memory and concentration. Let us consider this crisis a learning experience and invest now in a resilient future.

What I notice in practice is that individuals, companies and organizations are all searching far and wide for a way to accomplish this. It's far from obvious to put what I've described so far into practice, especially for people who have no experience with mental resilience. Moreover, investing in better minds is always custom work. Just as every individual, every company and every sector has its own needs and challenges, each one of them also has its own advantages and challenges when it comes to growing capital. And every crisis presents specific problems and therefore specific opportunities for growth. Although there are a number of basic rules and recommendations for empowering your brain, the steps involved must be tailor-made for each individual or company.

On the basis of the insights that research has given us over the last 20 years, we are now more able than ever to give shape to a brain strategy. Such a strategy will first have to transform our disrupted relationships with time, space and each other into positive partnerships. Our brain has to become the foundation once more, and not a ping-pong ball we smash wildly to and fro.

Just think of brain strategy like redecorating a room, in which our brain is the window through which light streams in. The strategy up to now has been to move the window so that it better suits the rest of the decor. But it doesn't work that way, really. We have to adjust our decor to accommodate the state of the window.

Instead of trying to change our brain relative to the context, we should make our strategy more brain-friendly. To stay with the metaphor of the room: we have to use the room when the light is shining through the window (better interaction with time), arrange the furniture so that it is optimally lit (better interaction with space) and receive guests where the light is (better interaction with each other). One last point concerns the window itself. If we never clean it, after a while it will admit very little light. If we don't hang curtains, the colors in the room will fade. Basic hygiene is also necessary for our brain if we want to cash in on our mental capital.

The 47-percent rule

Investing in present and absent time

. . . .

DOING MORE IN YOUR PRESENT TIME

Forty-seven percent of the time, we are not paying attention; rather, we are in an "unconscious state of consciousness," as I explained in the chapter on consciously engaging your consciousness (p. 87). For employers, the thought that their staff are mentally absent nearly half of the time is probably hard to swallow, but that's reality. Now, you can interpret this figure in two different ways. One way is to try and push this percentage as low as you can; the second way is by trying to make better use of "present" and "absent" time.

Finding and retaining focus is a daily challenge for many people today. We're continually confronted with distraction and that makes it difficult to keep our attention focused for any length of time. One of the most inspiring books on the subject I've read is by the American computer scientist Cal Newport. In his book *Deep Work* he describes how, by choosing focus, he succeeded in finishing six scientific publications per year in addition to doing research and writing popular books. Of course, not everyone aims so high, but I'm convinced that with most people there's room for improvement. If people are on average distracted for 47 percent of the time, that means there are also people for whom this percentage is higher (or even significantly higher).

But instead of trying to create more present time, it is more useful, according to most researchers, to do more in present time. That is, to put our present time to better use. "If people have wandering thoughts 47 percent of the time, that means they need it," Daniel Gilbert says.

This certainly doesn't mean that we should all work part-time. The unconscious half of the time is an essential part of the concentrated half. As I described it earlier, daydreaming is usually not a waste of time; rather, it is essential for archiving, processing, planning and ambitions. In other words, those who want to get more quality out of focus time have to start investing in absent time.

INVESTING IN FOCUS TIME

How exactly do you get more out of your present time? There are three relatively simple techniques that can generate positive results quickly: (1) make it short, (2) work with time goals, and (3) ask yourself the sitting question.

TECHNIQUE 1
Make it short

The problem of wandering thoughts is not that you have them, but that they don't come at the right moments. The most important method for occasionally keeping the door closed is by opening it yourself now and then. That is to say: limit focus time to a realistic amount and calculate in a time for not-conscious thinking afterwards.

The average attention span of an adult today is somewhere between 30 and 45 minutes. For people who multitask, it is considerably shorter (approximately ten minutes). Keeping this in mind when planning meetings, giving lectures and organizing courses is the first step. A good example of this are the TED talks, at which even the best speakers in the world can't be on stage for more than 20 minutes. Their motto: "Make it short."

Of course it is not always possible to keep everything super-short. For this reason, a second technique involves inserting a small boredom break. Allowing attention to flag for a moment during a lecture by adding a less-demanding passage, getting coffee during a meeting, hauling out agendas in the classroom... After all, research shows that a bit of boredom stimulates creativity and productivity.

Dividing time, and this is an important rule, does not mean that you have to change tasks every time. Serial multitasking (I mentioned this earlier) is always a bad idea. Moreover, trying to finish various tasks quickly elicits ego depletion or exhaustion of willpower. Instead of finishing a report while also answering e-mails, it is better to begin with the most mentally difficult task (finishing the report), even if this means that you can only check and answer your e-mails two or three hours later. The mental load should decrease with each task, and after each task it is important to take a short rest.

Another rule to follow when "timeboxing," as this technique is also known, is Miller's "seven plus or minus two" law. You cannot string endless blocks of concentration together. After four long blocks, you can add a maximum of three short blocks before you need a real break.

TECHNIQUE 2
Work with time goals

Not only should the focus time be short, it should also be clear from the beginning that it will be short. During a meeting, state at the outset when it will be over and what exactly you want to have accomplished by then. This gives those involved not only a content-related goal, but also a time-related goal, which is an important condition for flow. Teachers can also apply it by writing on the board as soon as they arrive what they want to have achieved by the end of the class.

You can also set yourself concentrated time goals. By assigning yourself a specific task to complete within half an hour, you quickly learn how to work in a way that is more focused. Setting an alarm (especially in the beginning) is also a good idea.

Exactly how long the successive periods of concentration have to be is something that everyone has to work out for him- or herself. The rule of thumb is to not make the concentrated time too short (half an hour) or the boring time too long (a couple of minutes). But don't be afraid if you cannot concentrate in the beginning for more than ten minutes. The more often you apply this technique, the more your concentrated time will lengthen of its own accord.

TECHNIQUE 3
Ask yourself the sitting question

A third way of getting more out of your focus time is by taking a concentrated attitude. Most people know that a straight back and lengthened neck help to avoid back problems. But what few people realize is that this posture is not only good for the back, it also ensures that our lungs are free to send oxygen to the brain, and for brain-workers this is essential. In addition, a concentrated posture also contributes psychologically to greater focus. Research into "embodied cognition" shows that the position of the body can have a decisive effect on our cognition. One study showed, for example, that increased muscular tension can result in greater willpower when making a decision.

But in addition to adopting a concentrated posture as we sit, there is a much more important technique for getting more focus out of the position of your body: the sitting question. With every task you assign yourself, every meeting or every class, ask yourself the question: "Do I have to sit while doing it?" For some tasks, such as writing, sitting is indeed easier, even essential. But often, sitting isn't really necessary.

If the sitting question can be answered in the negative and the task doesn't take too long, then it's almost always better to stay standing. In two areas in particular, I see many possibilities for this technique.

The first is education. Nowadays we expect children and young people to sit for eight hours a day, resulting in a great many physical side effects (such as back problems and obesity). But who says that children have to sit down in order to be able to listen? If nothing has to be written down, why shouldn't we let them stand up for half an hour? Didn't Aristotle walk around with his students while giving lectures?

You can also apply the sitting question to meetings. Not so much to brainstorming and thinking sessions, but certainly to the daily or weekly meetings that everyone wants to keep short but which always manage to go overtime. The "stand-up meeting" (of about 15 minutes) is a good alternative. Researchers at Washington University in St. Louis have recently discovered that such meetings also lead to more creativity and collaboration between those present.

INVEST IN DISTRACTION

Optimizing focus time is one thing. We can also get a lot out of the time in which we're not focused. It is important in this respect to make a distinction between time for boredom and time for relaxation.

TECHNIQUE 1
Make time for boredom

When our thoughts wander, we are strongly inclined to put on the brakes. Certainly in the case of undesired (repetitive) thoughts, it is a better idea to keep track of them and then release them later. As I noted earlier, our brain primarily uses recurring thoughts to let us know that we still have a task to finish. By responding to such a thought with "I'll think about that later," you actually put your brain at ease. It also means that you have created a bond of trust with yourself. You will have an easier time letting a thought go if you know you can indeed deal with it later. So decide for yourself when you will actually think about it and then defer that moment to the not-too-distant future. If you do this consistently, you can trust yourself and it will be easier to put thorny thoughts aside.

Another kind of wandering thoughts are the kind that seem to jump from one thing to another without a causal connection. These unfocused thoughts are not only important for processing all the information that inundates us in a single day, but also as a source of creativity. Giving the brain free rein for a moment while letting the mind wander is in other words an essential part of brain-work.

Now, how can you transform this mind wandering from a disadvantage (worrying, wasting time) into an advantage (creative solutions)? Here too, the most important thing is to try and exert more influence on the "when." Instead of always allowing yourself to be overtaken by wandering thoughts, you can steer them more actively (though never completely) by generating a context in which such thoughts naturally arise: boredom.

A little bit of boredom, as we have already seen, promotes the creative process. Instead of running to and fro the whole day and trying to maintain constant focus, build in some harmless boredom. A good moment for building in boredom is right after a period of highly concentrated focus, such as a brainstorming session or reading a report.

The most important thing at such moments is that we don't concentrate on something else. Watching a movie or reading a personal e-mail is not boring enough to encourage mind wandering. For this reason, it's good to seek out boredom in places where there is little distraction: in quiet rooms.

The activity that gets you dreaming is of course highly personal. Try to find out what it is and when you get your best ideas. Tidying up your office, taking letters to the post office, photocopying, hanging around in a waiting room or eating something are all great ways to divert your thoughts. One technique for mind wandering that has recently gained a lot of followers is doodling. In *The Doodle Revolution*, author Sunni Brown describes how doodles are a powerful way of to calm your mind and encourage creativity.

TECHNIQUE 2
Be unreachable for a while

In addition to boredom, as human beings we also have a great need for relaxation. On that score, there is also plenty of room for improvement in our society. The balance between work time and free time is gone. There is simply too much overlap. On the one hand, there is the phenomenon of overtime, but on the other (which I think is much worse), too many people are taking their work home with them.

Modern technology makes it possible for many brain-workers to work at any time of day, even long after they've left the office. In principle, this could have the positive effect of allowing people to choose more autonomously when they do their work. The system of "flextime" and "gliding schedules" has garnered an enormous amount of interest lately, and rightly so.

In practice, unfortunately, what happens is that people just work more hours. Research at the Radboud University of Nijmegen has shown that people who work from home are more sensitive to burnout. After their working day is over, they check their e-mail again or read the last chapter of a report, text a colleague, and so forth. The difference between work time and leisure time is so blurred that in the end all time becomes work time.

Professor of work psychology Frederik Anseel at Ghent University has been researching the so-called "new work" for a while. He is moderately positive about flexible work systems. Research shows, for example, that employees in a flexible system perform better on average, are more motivated and slightly more engaged. They also report a slightly lower than average level of stress. But these positive effects are less pronounced than is generally assumed, and he also points out that not everyone benefits from working at home. Some people function better in a classic nine-to-five environment.

The growing overlap between work time and private time is frequently discussed. In France, the right to disconnect from work became law as of January 1, 2017. Companies with more than 50 employees can no longer expect their employees to read e-mails after work. In Germany, too, since 2014 managers have been forbidden to call or e-mail staff after working hours, except in emergencies. A number of companies have jumped on the work-life balance bandwagon. For several years now, Volkswagen Germany has ensured that its Blackberry servers cannot send e-mails to employees after working hours. Only half an hour before the start of the next working day does the server "open" again.

Personally, I'm not a big fan of such measures. Instead, I think we should be striving for a more supple way of integrating work and life. I see a better solution in a time policy that is primarily oriented towards increasing employees' autonomy rather than just frantically struggling to stop the overlap. Many employees now feel that even at home, they can't choose when they do what. If the boss e-mails, they start to work. Only when we think it over do we realize that it's not the boss who decides that we have to work, it's the technology.

A financial director who approached me admitted that she had a difficult time with the pressure she felt from her fellow directors to be always reachable. Gradually she learned to determine for herself when she was contactable and when not, and to communicate this to her team. At the weekend, her smartphone is not in her coat pocket, unless she knows that an extremely urgent matter is being handled. On vacation, she leaves her smartphone at home. Only in the morning and late afternoon does she check once to see whether there are any urgent calls. She no longer allows work to creep into the rest of her private life, with less stress as a result.

Working at home successfully and happily is mainly a question of making agreements with yourself. At home, as at work, the same basic rules for focus time apply. That is: keep it short, focus and set clear goals.

INVEST IN A GOOD NIGHT'S SLEEP

A final – but for a resilient mind indispensable – step in dealing with time better is restoring healthy sleep time. Sleep has an enormous impact on both our physical and mental health. People who get enough sleep – for (young) adults, seven to nine hours of sleep is recommended – live longer, suffer less from heart and artery disease and have fewer stress-related problems. They are more creative, emotionally more balanced and have a longer attention span. A lack of sleep slows down the learning process, damages the memory, and increases the risk of depression and other mental disorders.

Almost all of us know the rules for healthy sleep habits: go to sleep at the same time as often as possible and get up at the same time too (even during the weekend); avoid alcohol, nicotine and caffeinated drinks three hours before bedtime; turn off your tablet/smartphone/TV an hour before you go to sleep; and so on. It sounds familiar. And yet most of us violate these rules all the time.

Not getting enough sleep has become an erroneous status symbol, says Arianna Huffington, founder of the renowned American news site *The Huffington Post*: "Working until midnight and then running around exhausted should be stigmatized instead of celebrated." According to her, sleep is the most direct path to success and the most important protection against burnout. In her book *The Sleep Revolution*, she describes how sleep deprivation undermines our professional, emotional and sexual lives – but also how things can be different. Huffington uses her own life as an example: she got through her own burnout by choosing not to multitask anymore, and to get more sleep. The impact on her life was so great that she later reformed her entire personnel policy. In the editorial offices of *The Huffington Post*, "nap rooms" were installed that, rumor has it, are always occupied. More and more often, I hear people confess that a power nap of 15 minutes revives them mentally and prepares them for the next task at work. Research at Saarland University has shown that a midday nap of 45 minutes makes your memory five times stronger. A Parisian study found that a power nap of ten minutes is sufficient to be more alert, and to reverse some negative effects of stress caused by lack of sleep.

Divide space and conquer

Choose focus in an infinite space

. . . .

PUTTING A STOP TO INFOBESITY

Today, more than ever, we move through an infinite space. Our work space extends far beyond the walls of our office into our living room and sometimes even our bedroom, via a wireless network that stretches to the other side of the world. In that space there is a continuous hum of information streams that greatly upsets the acoustics. How are we as human beings supposed to find flow in all this?

No one will that "the new work" and modern technologies form a new challenge to our brain. It is important that we adjust to the new reality of digitization, not by throwing all technology out the window, but by taking back control of our digital lives. Just as you don't fight obesity by locking the refrigerator, you don't fight infobesity by denying people access to information. Coping better with the infinity of space today is mainly about (re)claiming freedom of choice: over what part of that space we use when, and also over the way in which we want to use that space.

DIVIDING SPACE: THE IMPORTANCE
OF PHYSICAL AND MENTAL DOORS

To be able to choose again which part of space we use, we have to start at the beginning: the division of space. Today, most people's spaces run together. As with furnishing a loft, you start by dividing the space into smaller units by giving each unit a different function (kitchen, bathroom, bedroom, living room, work area); but we can also do this with our minds. This is not to say that each part of the space has to be hermetically sealed from the rest – it doesn't hurt to let the air out now and then – but it should be possible once again to be present in only one room if we so wish.

We encounter a very concrete example of this at the office. The idea of an open office, in which everyone is directly connected to each other and the world, is ideal for promoting collaboration and dialogue, but is completely unsuitable for concentrated work. According to neuropsychiatrist Theo Compernolle, author of the bestseller *Brain Chains*, an open office reduces employees' efficiency by as much as 40 percent. The biggest problem of open offices is the excess of auditory stimuli, especially the phone conversations of coworkers. An American study showed that a brief interruption of around three seconds led to employees making twice as many mistakes, even when they had to type two digits. Even worse, it takes an average of 25 minutes before we can completely resume a task after being disturbed, at least according to Tom DeMarco, co-author of *Peopleware*, a book about productivity that is in its third edition. When the task is complex, you can add another 15 minutes before we achieve the same initial focus. And I suspect that during that time span we'll already have been disturbed again ...

In other words, an open office is not suitable for every business. It would also be good if entrepreneurs considered the pros and cons rather than just falling for the hype. Do you expect your employees to consult one another or do they need to be able to work undisturbed in a concentrated way? The answer will help determine how best to organize your office space.

At most companies and institutions, meetings are held and people also work in a concentrated way. Ideally, this combination is reflected in the office space and separate areas are provided for both functions. Of course not everyone is able to completely reorganize their office, but there will always be solutions for those who seek them. The creation of a single quiet room, for example, where no technology is admitted, can be a major step forward.

At schools, physically dividing space into "streaming rooms" (where information may flow freely) and "quiet rooms" (where no technology is allowed) can make a world of difference. At present, most schools work with one of these two systems: they either prohibit all technology or embrace it wholeheartedly. The first system ensures that students will crave their devices even more, without learning how to deal with them in a healthy way. In the second, concentration is often the first victim: students are continually distracted by all kinds of messages and status updates.

I think it's not necessary to have to choose between the two systems; a better idea would be to give the teachers and the students who use the spaces more choice. By offering both possibilities, we teach children and young people that each system has its pros and cons. They can find out for themselves how certain functions (such as reading and solving problems) are better carried out in a quiet space, while others (such as gathering knowledge and being creative) are better in lively spaces. A survey of high-school students conducted by trend agency Trendwolves shows that a large number of students are, in fact, requesting more peace and quiet in the classroom.

Dividing space according to function is not just a physical matter. We also have to install mental doors that we can close at appropriate moments. One new challenge in this area is working at home, which I discussed earlier. Working at home erodes boundaries: we take our work home and our home to work.

More and more companies allow their staff to work at home at least a couple of days a week. Worldwide this percentage is still low: around six percent, but internationally, the differences are considerable. The United States are the frontrunners in this area, with around 40 percent of the working population. In Belgium, the figure is around 27 percent. In the Netherlands, only 13 percent. A lot also depends on the sector and the position of the employee, but everything points to the number of telecommuters increasing considerably over the next decade.

Although the opportunity is offered with increasing frequency, employers rarely invest in the work area at home. What percentage of those working at home simply sit at the kitchen table? And isn't it strange that companies that spend millions on modern office spaces scarcely consider the way in which a quarter of their employees work at home?

As for the way space is organized, we as individuals don't always have much input. So it's important to invest in learning how better to cope with the infinite space in which we live. Many people feel they can't choose where to direct their thoughts or attention, and that they are increasingly sucked into several (sometimes dozens) of spaces at a time. Social networks and mobile apps inundate us with information, opinions, facts, challenges and thoughts. Our brain, desperately searching for a way to process all this, starts multitasking. And that's the problem.

In the scientific world it is a well-known fact that people can't multitask. We might think it's a pity, but the research is unanimous: people cannot do two things at once. And no, before you start: women can't either.

It seems strange in a world in which doing one thing at a time seems like pure luxury. Who doesn't listen to the radio while driving a car? And can't we all phone and walk at the same time, or text while watching television? At least we think we can. But in reality our brain never does two things at exactly the same time.

If we oblige our brain to multitask, there are actually only two possibilities. One is that our brain shuts down consciousness for one activity. In the case of phoning while walking, we do the latter on pure autopilot. But if we try to combine two activities that require our attention, the brain has no choice but to shuttle back and forth between the two tasks. We think we can text while watching a film, but in reality we never do both at the same time. And the more closely the tasks are related (such as writing an e-mail while talking), the slower the switch.

Although scientists labeled multitasking nonsense ages ago, we we all still believe in it. With all the consequences. To start with, multitasking does not help us work faster – it actually slows us down. Research shows that when you're performing a task, such as reading a report, but are then distracted by an e-mail, it takes an average of 25 minutes before your complete attention is once again focused on reading the report. Multitaskers are moreover up to 40 percent less productive and significantly less creative. Research on young people who studied in front of the television shows that this combination results in the incoming knowledge being stored in the wrong part of the brain, so that they cannot make active use of it. Multitaskers have a harder time finishing their tasks and make more mistakes. Multitasking has a negative effect on your memory, your IQ and even your relationships. Combining eating with another task is harmful to your health and working on several tasks at once causes physical stress.

Multitasking is the true enemy of a better mind. Each and every one of the resources I discussed in Part II of this book (self-control, consciously engaging your consciousness, focus and optimism) suffers if we try to combine tasks. Our focus gets lost, it becomes impossible to process new information consciously, we lose our self-control and it makes us unhappier to boot.

The most important cause of the multitasking crisis we are now experiencing is no secret: the technological revolution. When Sandra Bond Chapman, founder of the Center for Brain Health at the University of Texas, asks people today when their best brain years were, they consistently refer (regardless of age) to a period around ten or 20 years ago: the period before mobile phones and computers took over.

Since the 1990s, we have started multitasking en masse, while the pile of proof that multitasking doesn't work has reached mountainous proportions. And thus the question arises: If we know all this, why do we keep doing it? Neuroscientists have discovered the answer to that too: we multitask because we are addicted to it.

The multitasking addiction prevails at different levels. First, it gives us a feeling of satisfaction because it seems (at least for a while) as if we're doing well. Second (apparently), efficient multitaskers get a lot of credit in our society, and as human beings we are highly susceptible to praise. But finally, we are also literally addicted to multitasking.

With "successful" multitasking, the reward system in our brain is activated in such a way that it releases dopamine, the happiness hormone. This flood of dopamine makes you feel so good that you really believe you're working efficiently. It encourages you to continue your multitasking habit, which in turn releases a new shot of dopamine, and so on. Multitaskers become addicted to this dopamine and constantly seek out new stimuli that will cause a brief dopamine rush.

The financial, societal, social and mental price of multitasking is huge, but the market has become so big thanks to this collective addiction that technology companies have no choice but to respond to this dependence. Not coincidentally, the latest technological gadgets promise to make multitasking easier. For example, I'm thinking of multi-device keyboards, with which you can operate several computers at once, or iFusion, with which you can control all your Apple devices at the same time.

Gadgets like these simplify multitasking on a practical level only. In our brain, they only create more barriers and less efficiency. What disturbs (and astonishes) neuroscientists most of all is that repeated multitasking doesn't make us better at multitasking – it makes us worse. A study by Stanford University showed that multitaskers performed complex tasks more poorly than singletaskers because they had more difficulty organizing their thoughts and filtering out irrelevant information. Moreover, the multitaskers were slower when switching between two tasks. For a long time, it was thought that this cognitive deterioration from multitasking was temporary. But research at the University of Sussex suggests otherwise: the brains of multitaskers exhibited less dense gray matter in the anterior cingulate cortex, an area that is responsible for empathy and cognitive and emotional control.

It goes from bad to worse. Young people who have grown up with mobile phones and computers are worse at combining tasks than the generation that experienced the analog age. A well-known saying in this regard is: "If Steve Jobs had had an iPad as a child, he would never have invented one." Apparently Jobs was convinced of this himself, because he wouldn't let his children use his devices and limited their Internet usage.

Hopefully, it has now become clear that you must use your mental space as well and as efficiently as possible. But how do you do that in concrete terms? Here, too, I would like to propose a number of practical techniques.

TECHNIQUE 1
Stop multitasking

This is certainly not a plea in favor of banning all technology from your life and going back to the time when you had to accomplish everything via a single landline. What I'm arguing for is using technology more wisely. Don't let technology eat away at your mind; rather, use your mind to make full use of technological capabilities.

The first and most important step is also the most radical: stop multitasking and begin singletasking. The most obvious way to do this is to try not to combine tasks anymore. In most offices and even domestic spaces, everything is oriented towards combining tasks. Think of all the laptop meetings at work or the open kitchens that allow parents to help the kids with their homework while preparing a meal. And how many desks are turned towards the television to make doing homework more pleasant?

If two reports have to be finished on the same day, most people will work a little on the first, then a little on the second, then a bit more on the first, and so on. In this way, you probably feel like you're doing well, because both reports do indeed seem to be progressing. In reality, however, you progress much more slowly than if you completed one report after the other. If you have two days in which to finish two reports, you'll be doing yourself a favor if you set two deadlines and do each report on a different day instead of trying to do them both at once.

Most people can let go of this sort of multitasking fairly easily, especially if they understand what it's costing them. What's harder is resisting stimuli from our environment.

This is the kind of multitasking to which we are especially addicted today.

Our computer screen is a good example of how context stimulates us to multitask. Most people have lots of folders on their desktop, most of which they don't have to open very often in practice. At the bottom or side of the screen is an icon bar that depicts all the programs available. So while you're working, you're regularly reminded of all the things you can do. Before they start work, most people open their e-mail, Internet, social network sites and diary as a matter of course – all programs that give visual or audio signals whenever a new message comes in. In addition, most people leave their mobile lying on their desk, and in some cases a paper diary as well.

What are the things that distract you when you have to perform an important task? And to what extent do you permit these distractions, and what effect do they have on your efficiency? Today we have become so accustomed to distraction that it doesn't even seem to bother us anymore. But of course it does. Every time a message arrives, an alarm goes off, a news item captures our attention, we lose our concentration and it takes effort and mental energy to return to the task we were engaged in.

TECHNIQUE 2
First the elephants, then the rabbits

While you are working on an important assignment, it is important to cut off outside lines. No social media, telephone or e-mail to constantly distract us. For our productivity and for our brain, this is undoubtedly a good choice, but in a context that is so driven by multitasking, it is not always easy to put this into practice. Actually, everyone with whom you interact should not only be aware of your decision to be unreachable, but should also agree that you won't be answering your phone or your e-mails if you're finishing a task. Unfortunately, in many cases this is impossible to achieve. Therefore, I advise people to follow another strategy: prioritize.

Confronted with a large amount of work, many people are inclined to make to-do lists to be sure they haven't forgotten anything. But this strategy doesn't work as well as could be hoped. The big problem with to-do lists is that they don't distinguish between large and small tasks. By mixing everything together, we convince our brain that we can finish all tasks in random order. And then what do we do automatically? We'll start with the smallest and move up.

This way, it does indeed seem as if you're working through your to-do list at top speed, at least in the beginning. You cross out or check off things on your smartphone. But at some point you reach the big tasks and then the fun stops. Not only does it take more time to finish, but you also have less mental and physical energy to finish the last (big) tasks, so that you often postpone them.

As human beings, we are strongly inclined to choose the "quick reward," as we saw previously in the chapter on self-control (see p. 61). For this reason, we almost automatically choose to do the small tasks first. The problem is that this strategy contributes to "ego depletion," or the exhaustion of willpower (see p. 81), such that our self-control is compromised. And what is the result? We risk procrastination.

In addition, we are very bad at estimating how long a specific task will take. We consistently underestimate the time needed for "short assignments," and usually overestimate how much time a "long assignment" will take.

A typical example is answering e-mails. Most people start their working day by opening their mailbox and reading new messages. Sound familiar? You probably also answer a few of those messages right away, which in itself is time-consuming. It becomes really problematic when you try to finish a large assignment and in the meantime keep answering e-mails one after another. The result? You feel like you're drowning in work and that you'll never finish anything. Your head is everywhere and nowhere. You feel like a juggler who has to keep several balls in the air, which adds stress. This is how multitasking eventually leads to reduced engagement.

A possible solution to this problem lies in splitting the day into priorities and small tasks, and then working through them in that order: first the elephants, then the rabbits. This animal metaphor comes from a pronouncement by the Texan oil magnate and millionaire Thomas Boone Pickens: "When you are hunting elephants, don't get distracted chasing rabbits." You could see the elephants as priorities on the horizon, which you have to hunt strategically. The rabbits are hopping around everywhere, and you could end up hunting them willy-nilly, like the effect of letting the issues of the day sweep you along in their wake.

The principle is actually quite simple. Instead of making a to-do list, start each day with ten minutes in which you choose the "elephant of the day" (or up to three smaller elephants). By placing a small number of tasks first, you foster focused attention. Having a clear goal in mind is one of the most important conditions for flow.

Moreover, this strategy gives you the opportunity to give yourself a reward: the rabbits. After you've finished that one elephant, you can reward yourself by doing some small tasks. Checking e-mails, making a few phone calls or straightening out your paperwork – all in a single block of time. As a prize for all that hard work, it might sound pretty poor, but that's not how it feels in reality. As we have seen, the brain releases a certain amount of dopamine upon the completion of each task, which gives us a good feeling. This is what makes checking off those "rabbits" so satisfying.

Nearly all the people who applied this strategy at my recommendation are satisfied with the results. They have seen their own efficiency and productivity increase, while also getting a great feeling of satisfaction. The technique also ensures that they finish their important tasks when they're physically and mentally most energetic: usually in the morning. For this reason, most people have an easier time achieving flow with this strategy.

This strategy is also applicable to our entire working week. Put the elephants that you definitely want to finish by the end of the week at the front. And of course the list can change over time. Although a simple list is not that useful, a dynamic to-do list is. Determine your priorities daily, weekly, and over the long term, but also be flexible enough to adjust them as circumstances change, or when something urgent crops up.

Some people couple their intention to ward off all distraction during their "elephant time" by hanging a sign on the door – sometimes with an elephant poster if this philosophy is familiar to the company in question – or by switching off the telephone and e-mail or simply by using earplugs. Decide for yourself which distractions keep you from your priorities and try your best to eliminate them.

TECHNIQUE 3
Create screen-free time

We don't just multitask at work – we also do it in our free time, and at home we're often busy doing several things at once. A scene that everyone is familiar with is a couple sitting in a restaurant while they both play with their smartphones. Just because we carry the world in our pocket doesn't mean we have to whip it out all the time, everywhere we go – but that's exactly what we do.

Whenever we use technology, we live our lives less intensely, making it difficult to get satisfaction out of the moment. Because we're always busy with other things, memories don't last as long. And because we always give in to the temptation to check for new messages, we also lose our self-control more often and "grit" becomes difficult to achieve. In short, we find life less enjoyable when we try to do everything at once.

If we want to live more fully again, we need to incorporate "screen breaks" into our lives. Moments in which we are not constantly invited to answer this message or that phone call. Moments in which we are consciously doing something, but also moments in which we can give our thoughts freedom to roam in the infinite. And this is only possible when our attention is not attracted by a blinking smartphone or computer screen.

SINGLETASKING VERSUS BURNOUT

The multitasking crisis is not solely to blame on technology; it also has to do with changed expectations in business. Today, staff are above all expected to be "flexible" and "multifunctional." In the first chapter, we saw how all these demands can cause "role stress" among employees. More and more people have a difficult time describing their own job function and defining their tasks. Flexible, multifunctional employees almost always have several projects going on at once and try to work on them all at the same time. This kind of multitasking fosters even more role stress. And role stress – as I've said before – is one of the most important causes of burnout.

Of course, it's no coincidence that burnout crops up with a vengeance in times of recession. Companies have to save money – including on personnel – so that the remaining employees are given extra tasks that have nothing to do with their own specialty. That doesn't necessarily have to be a problem. On the contrary – in the most positive interpretation, this kind of operation presents employees with new challenges, boosts creativity and yields new insights. And that's how it can be, on the condition that tasks do indeed remain separate tasks.

Because this kind of operation is usually set in motion out of necessity, executives almost never use the opportunity to get the most out of the situation. Learning to singletask is an asset for everyone, but especially for employees with complex functions. In an ideal scenario, an employee only begins a set of tasks after he or she has received a complete description of the job and clear agreements have been made about which assignments happen when. It would not be out of place, for example, to agree that each project be worked on at regular intervals.

It's not at all lonely at the top

Motivation in connection

. . . .

STIMULATING COOPERATION

The age-old truism that successful people are happier and therefore have more social relationships has been increasingly called into question in both neuroscience and psychology. The reverse seems to be closer to the truth: people with many social relationships are happier and therefore more successful.

For our psychological well-being as well as our sense of engagement, the importance of our interaction with and connection to others has long been underestimated. Even though we've known for some time that networking is essential to moving up and that collaboration pays, we still seem to fall into the trap of egoism in businesses, institutions and organizations. That it's every man for himself in this world (where, remember, it's lonely at the top), doesn't change the fact that we need each other. A brain-friendly strategy inevitably addresses this primal need for connection by stimulating interaction and cooperation, also improving executives' communication skills.

For the government, connection between citizens is by definition a point of interest. This isn't an ambition to cash in on mental capital as much as a desire to limit social problems related to exclusion and loneliness, such as suicide, radicalization, crime and mental disorders.

In education, attention is traditionally paid to cooperation and interaction. A recent – and in my opinion highly welcome – addition to this strategy are programs against bullying. In psychology, the effects of bullying on children are well known. Bullies at school have significantly more chance of becoming criminals as adults, but research also shows that the victims still carry the social, physical and mental consequences as much as 40 years later. The silent group in a class where bullying takes place also has less chance of benefiting from their mental capital.

Although in education, as in the public sector, there is still room for improvement, it is clear that the business world has the most potential for growth in this area. Team-building activities are one of the few ways in which connection between colleagues is stimulated at most companies today. These kinds of activities are undoubtedly conducive to a positive atmosphere at work. They can contribute to a feeling of group solidarity among employees and a sense of connection beyond the workplace, which is an important strategy for combating burnout. But it's just one of the options.

During the business training courses we offer, we usually go a step further and often work with pairs, or buddies. In the process we let people cooperate very consciously on a particular task during training, but especially over the long term. Realizing cooperation as a goal in a company not only creates a sense of connection with each other, but also with the company. It goes without saying that this doesn't always go smoothly, but a lot can be learned from confrontation.

Another possibility is giving team-building activities a new twist. For example, one day a year, as a company allow all employees to think outside the box, create groups, and think up and work out new ideas for the company. The best idea is then put into practice the following year. Another example is that employees challenge one another to reach a specific sports goal, such as running a company marathon or organizing a softball tournament.

More communal (work) activities do not necessarily lead to better connections. For this to succeed, a significant shift in mentality is often needed. I like to refer to the work of Brené Brown, who, in her influential book *The Power of Vulnerability*, also argues for another way of working (and living). According to her, we live in a society that forces us to wear a mask of perfection. If you want to be successful, it seems that it's important not to show your insecurities. Brown, however, says that we must embrace uncertainty and vulnerability as a force. Only then is it possible to arrive at true connection, and this can only have positive effects in the long term.

TO Y OR NOT TO Y?

One particular challenge for connectedness at the workplace is intergenerational cooperation. Soon, for the first time, we will have four generations working together. When "generation Z" (born after 1995) enters the workforce, the babyboomers (born before 1965) will still be working, as will the generations in between (generations X and Y).

In 2025, 75 percent of the labor market will consist of people from generation Y. But the number of those over 50 is also increasing. Cooperating with people from different generations is a hot topic for every company. Generations have different norms and values, but also different competences. There is thus a need for intergenerational management. Or to put it simply: for cooperating with people from different generations.

Aging is not the biggest problem. It is the way we deal with it. For older generations, it's an art to remain open to the fact that young people are evolutionarily better at cooperating. They are more open to fresh ideas, to updates. But young people also need to understand that older people can bring their knowledge and experience to those fresh ideas. If you are ready to enter into dialogue, you as a group stand an excellent chance.

The principle of "recognized inequality" is crucial in this respect. Everyone has strengths and weaknesses. This recognition is the basis of complementary cooperation. We need to employ people on the basis of their strengths. And as colleagues, to understand, esteem and utilize the positive contributions of every generation.

BRAIN-FRIENDLY COMMUNICATION

Brain-friendly business communication is communication that takes into account the way employees receive and process messages. The key concepts here are setting a good example, feedback and formulating goals.

Every positive policy begins with a positive attitude on the part of the company's executives. An executive not only makes clear in words what is expected of employees, but also (and perhaps most of all) in deeds. It is therefore essential for an executive to set a good example.

That sounds logical, of course, but all too often I see executives who want to invest in their employees minds stumble on this point. Many high-ranking individuals have the habit of being the last to leave work, and never take breaks – even if they don't expect the same of their staff. This inconsistency exacts its toll, however, because it saddles employees with a double message. As an executive you can say that you don't expect employees to answer e-mails after 6pm, but as long as you keep doing it yourself, that message won't get through.

A second component of better communication is the clear determination of goals. According to flow psychologist Mihaly Csikszentmihalyi, many executives make the mistake of explaining what the goal of the company is, but forgetting to say what specific role they have assigned each employee. But having a clear goal in mind is essential to finding focus and generating flow. Those who don't really know what they're doing are more subject to role stress, which is a predictor for burnout. In a team where you have to arrive at an end product together, it is important to give each employee goals, so that he or she can see the result and therefore also be held responsible for it. This is why when starting a new project, it's so important not only to introduce the project itself, but also the strategy for realizing it and the methods of implementation involved.

A third important part of brain-friendly communication is investing in feedback. Receiving immediate feedback, according to Csikszentmihalyi, is crucial for generating engagement and flow. Conversely, a lack of feedback causes a person's motivation to decrease significantly. Over the long term this can even lead to burnout. Moreover, executives who don't give feedback rarely get what they really want.

Try as much as possible to make feedback a habit – for example, by opting for regular feedback moments, preferably several times a year. Don't just plan occasional feedback conversations when things aren't going well, because employees will soon feel that they only receive feedback if they've made a mistake. This gives feedback a bad name. If you schedule regular feedback conversations and keep positive feedback in mind, negative remarks will be more readily accepted.

As an individual, it's important to be open to the feedback you get from your colleagues. It isn't always easy to handle criticism, but if the criticism is meant constructively, you can see feedback as an important resource. If you feel you're getting little or no feedback, initiate a conversation about it. It never hurts to ask your supervisor to evaluate your performance.

In the best cases, feedback not only follows quickly on performance, it also takes into account the rules of constructive criticism. Good feedback is simple, clear and comprehensible on all levels. Avoid ambiguous language and give highly concrete, workable examples on points that can be improved. Very important: be sure to emphasize strengths as well. What you as an executive must avoid at all costs is feedback that is open to interpretation because you have used vague or emotional terms ... "I'm quite satisfied, but you are underperforming" is an example. Instead, indicate very clearly what is good, what needs improvement and how your employee can do this.

It would be a good thing for mental resilience if simple communication in words and matching actions reappeared in the business world. Today, many executives communicate in another unit – money. A survey conducted by psychologists Teresa Amabile and Steven Kramer at the Harvard Business School revealed that 95 percent of CEOs are convinced that money is the most important reason why people work. However, their study is completely at odds with this theory. It's not money but emotions that are the main reason people work, especially the feeling of making a bit of progress every day. This phenomenon is known as the Progress Principle.

Not only is money not such a strong motivator, several researchers have shown that financial rewards are generally counterproductive. Motivation psychology explains why this is so. Bonuses, incentives and rewards cause the intrinsic motivation of employees (you work hard and well because you enjoy your work) to decrease and replace it with an external motivation (you work hard and well because you want to earn a bonus). And once the reward is given, it is expected every time in greater and greater quantity. Bestselling business author Dan Pink even says: "The greater the financial reward, the worse the performance." He argues that businesses can win the loyalty of their intrinsically motivated employees better with high fixed wages than with bonuses or incentives, which only result in employees trying to finish their work faster in order to get the bonus.

This scientific finding has major implications for the business world. Incentives are now so established in certain sectors that it might seem difficult to make changes. Still, there are strategies that companies can use in order to reward employees without affecting their motivation.

The first way is to give employees as much autonomy as possible and sufficient room for making individual decisions. Research on happiness has shown that autonomy is one of the most important predictors of happiness at work. By leaving certain decisions to individual employees, you as a manager delegate responsibility. This creates a feeling of trust, and trust is a much safer basis for performance than (unreliable) rewards. Moreover, increased autonomy means that completed assignments feel like "achievements," so that employees can be more satisfied with their work.

How this works exactly was demonstrated several years ago by Alaska Airlines. When the turnover of the airline took a downturn, management developed a new strategy in which employee autonomy played a significant part. Employees were given more freedom to act at their discretion and seek solutions for passengers who had missed their flight or had problems with their luggage. Most airlines are hesitant to grant this kind of decision-making power to their service staff and work out strict protocols to which their employees must adhere. This often has negative consequences, as no two passengers at the check-in counter are the same. Where a standardized approach might be fine for customer A, it only adds fuel to the fire for customer B. At such moments the check-in clerk can feel completely powerless – he may understand what the customer wants and see a way to help, but according to the rules he's not allowed to. For Alaska Airlines, the experiment turned out to be a success. Not only were the employees highly satisfied, but the company got a reputation for being very customer-oriented and increased its turnover considerably.

A second strategy is to invest in positive and constructive feedback. Research shows that having the feeling of making progress is one of the most important reasons why people work. By giving consistent feedback, people are encouraged to improve themselves even more.

This finding is not only vital for corporate life, it also has considerable implications for education. According to American author Alfie Kohn, "If you do this, you'll get that" is one of the most harmful sentences ever to invade education and pedagogy. But teachers are also urged to "reward rather than punish" children as much as possible. Admittedly, punishment still seems to be more harmful to motivation than reward, but in education as in business, rewards have little or no positive effect.

Not only teachers, but also parents make liberal use of presents to get their children to study. A survey among Flemish students revealed, for example, that eight out of ten parents rewarded a good report card. In that same survey, it also appeared that only one quarter of the students actually worked harder with the promise of a reward. But even if they did study harder, they did it only for the sake of the reward and not because they wanted to intrinsically.

ENGAGED MOTIVATION

Motivation is a key concept in dealings between people. We adjust our own behavior largely to the behavior of others. In other words, we have to stimulate pupils, company employees and citizens to enter into our story by orienting their conduct towards our own.

As I pointed out in the second part of this book, our ability to control our own behavior is shaped by four principles: delayed gratification, intrinsic motivation, self-regulation and the limits of ego depletion. Those who want to motivate people cannot get around these principles.

You create engagement by making the resources for these four principles greater than the demands you make on them. Engagement expert Professor Arnold Bakker gives five ways to positively motivate employees: (1) offer a challenge, (2) ensure social support, (3) give feedback, (4) ensure that different skills are used and (5) give opportunities to grow and develop. Of course, it's also true that for each of these resources, there should be a healthy balance. Challenges, for example, will only be motivating if they are clearly defined, feasible, and if there is sufficient support provided along the way. If you're faced with a mountain of work that you will never be able to finish alone, this will be harmful to your motivation. If you know you can rely on the expertise of your colleagues to bring a challenging task to a successful conclusion, the mountain of work feels completely different. The same is true for varying tasks and capabilities: employees who are required to combine different skills are often more satisfied because they get a lot of variety in their daily work, but if they have to do too many different things at the same time, there is a danger of role stress and multitasking. As always, an important condition is that you also respect the limits of ego depletion. Too many assignments one after another are detrimental to self-control and hence also to the motivation of your employees.

WHY YOU CAN'T CONSIDER MOTIVATION
APART FROM FLOW

When conducting his research, flow psychologist Mihaly Csikszentmihalyi looked for more than just engagement: flow. In this state of positive, concentrated attention, our brain works optimally. Engagement is an important condition for flow and arises under comparable circumstances. Csikszentmihalyi identified three conditions for flow.

The first condition is a clear and achievable goal. This is closely related to the first principle of self-control: belief in delayed gratification. In any case, it is important according to both Bakker and Csikszentmihalyi that not only the main goal is explicit (for example, getting a diploma in education), but that the intermediate goals (mastering each subject) are also clear, and that the person in question clearly knows what is expected of him or her.

The second condition is clearly related to the first: feedback. In addition to the classic top-down feedback, many companies are also starting to work with what is known as 360-degree feedback, in which all colleagues, regardless of their position, are evaluated by one another. This not only encourages employee motivation, it also gives them a greater feeling of responsibility. It is also important that this happens in a safe and constructive professional atmosphere: you shouldn't feel that your feedback will be used against you later.

A third condition for flow is challenge. This means not only that the assignment has to have a certain level of difficulty, but above all that it doesn't feel like a requirement or an obligation. You can see there is a connection here to the importance of autonomy and freedom of choice, both particularly important factors when it comes to work satisfaction and happiness on the job.

Our optimal brain
A strategy for better minds

. . . .

A BRAIN-FRIENDLY STRATEGY
VERSUS A BRAIN STRATEGY

S mall changes in our environment can have major effects on our resilience. But if we really want to empower our brain, we have to go for a real brain strategy, not
just a brain-friendlier strategy. In businesses and schools, certainly, but I also see a major role for the government to play.

At present, there is no talk of such a strategy at any level.
Although various governments – including Belgium's – have
taken the first tentative steps towards stemming the tide of
burnout and other stress-related problems, policy is still restricted to hesitant attempts by isolated individuals. In the
programs of political parties, mental health is not a priority.
The recognition of burnout as a malady is a first step in the
right direction, but without a supporting policy it remains a
drop in the ocean.

Nevertheless, our brains could still use some extra attention. Thanks to psychology and neurology, we know now better than ever what kind of attention is needed to optimize
our cognitive capabilities. Research into neuroplasticity, the
changeability of our brain, is still in the process of development, but a number of things have already become clear.
Not only children but also adults can significantly increase
their brain capacity through training and development,-
so that they become happier and more attentive, and also

show more impulse control. Apparently, we may gradually start to consider character and intelligence as capacities instead of innate characteristics.

A positive brain strategy is a strategy that invests in the development of these capacities. There are a number of paths that can be taken. In the first place, awareness is required. By informing people of the importance of good brain hygiene, many difficulties can be prevented. It can also encourage people to take charge themselves and look for ways to empower their brain. In addition, a brain strategy could also give people more access to existing training programs by removing thresholds or by providing the training itself.

AWARENESS BUILDING

Since the 1990s, interest in the brain has increased exponentially, but mental health nevertheless remains taboo in many places. Organizations and businesses that really want to invest in a brain strategy must begin by building awareness. A strategy can only be successful if everyone joins in the story.

On the one hand, the government has a very clear responsibility in this respect when it comes to getting the ball rolling. But businesses can also take on the role of social entrepreneurs by conducting awareness campaigns among their own employees. An important step in the right direction has already been taken by the "Big Four" of professional service networks, Deloitte, EY, KPMG and PricewaterhouseCoopers (PwC). Deloitte was the first of the four to build up a program around resilience. After senior partner John Binns was confronted with depression in 2007, he became head of the Mental Health Champions Programme in the United Kingdom, which he uses to set up top-down campaigns. At PwC, employees have had the option for several years now of signing up for a course on the anticipation and prevention of burnout. KPMG entered into a "mental health charter" with its employees, and EY has been working on a "mental health buddy" system in recent years, in which employees with mental health difficulties can request assistance through an informal network. Of course, these businesses, which employ tens of thousands of people in a sector that is highly vulnerable to burnout, still have a lot further to go. What makes me particularly optimistic is that not only the Big Four but also other companies have clearly chosen to conduct positive campaigns. Too many businesses focus on working out a campaign around mental health that resembles the prevention of an illness. But prevention (trying to ensure that problems don't arise) needs to be coupled with anticipation (preparing the reaction to problems). Moreover, we can make people enthusiastic by paying particular attention to the way mental and cognitive health can contribute to more success, happiness and engagement.

Awareness building does not always have to happen through programs and campaigns. Role models can also play an important part. CEOs, HR managers and other executives and teachers can all make a significant contribution. People like Bill Schlegel, executive director of EY, who made mental health an acceptable topic of discussion within his company after his wife committed suicide. People like Arianna Huffington, who goes radically against the grain with her personnel policy. These people can be rightly regarded as pioneers.

In addition to speaking out, an even more important role awaits executives who set a good example themselves. When you sweep the stairs, you always start at the top and work your way down. And as I mentioned earlier, the example an executive sets is often more important than what comes out of his or her mouth. An employer who encourages his employees not to think about work at home should not be sending e-mails at five in the morning.

Building awareness about the importance of a resilient mind is urgently needed in the world of education too. Since study after study confirms that it is not intelligence and knowledge but rather perseverance, focus and optimism that determine the success – and hence the future – of students, we must be able to create a space for them in education. A number of prominent figures have also called for a thorough reform of education in this respect.

One of the best-known proponents of this theme is the American economist James Heckman, who won the Nobel Prize for economics in 2000. In publications and lectures, Heckman tries to convince the world that our education system wrongly attaches too much importance to measuring intelligence and knowledge, while it should actually focus on self-control. Matthieu Ricard also says: "Happiness is a skill, emotional balance is a skill, compassion and altruism are skills and just like all skills they need to be developed through education." Author Paul Tough, in his book *How Children Succeed*, says that it is time to replace the "cognitive hypothesis" (that success is a result of intelligence and knowledge) with the "character hypothesis" (that success lies in grit and curiosity).

Strengthening the mind affects how a child is able to "start" in life. It has an effect on school performance, career opportunities and later income, but also on psychological well-being: mental disorders are considerably reduced by investing in a strong and resilient mind from childhood onwards. Another consequence is that it reduces the chance of behavioral problems, which in turn reduces crime as well as the healthcare costs for that person. In short, both the individual and society will benefit from investments made in strengthening the minds of our children and youth.

Brain training is gradually trickling into education. In the United States, good results have been obtained with children from disadvantaged neighborhoods, who, thanks to brain training, scored better on their admissions exams for higher education in comparison to other children from the same neighborhoods who received placebo training.

In education, I think there is a great deal of potential in introducing a "brain hour." In addition to measures to make classes, teaching methods and lesson content brain-friendlier, we should prepare children and young people for a resilient future by introducing "mental education" along with "physical education." Becoming aware of and training cognitive skills as well as traits such as self-control and grit can deliver a considerable advantage in a short amount of time. A Canadian study has shown that a mindfulness program for children in primary school resulted not only in progress with respect to their social-emotional skills, but also in better mathematics scores. In the long run, we can create a generation that is more resilient and can cope with stressors more flexibly.

In addition, there is also the Penn Resiliency Program, which, as its name suggests, invests in resilience. This program was developed by a team of psychologists at the University of Pennsylvania. The goal of the program is to strengthen children's resilience, optimistic thinking, coping strategies and problem-solving abilities so as to increase their psychological well-being, but also to improve their behavior, attendance and academic abilities. The effectiveness of this program was tested in several countries. In the Netherlands, the first results are trickling in. One study shows that teenage girls who showed elevated depression scores at the beginning of the study showed a decrease in symptoms of depression after the program.

Finally, the research team of Professor Richard Davidson – the man who put the monk Ricard in the scanner – recently presented the results of their "kindness curriculum" among four- and five-year-olds. These toddlers spent 12 weeks doing exercises to make them more aware of themselves and others. Through exercises that drew their attention to the here and now, the children were better able to place their emotions, were more attentive and nicer to others. Moreover, they also scored considerably better on academic skills. These toddlers had a better sense of "delayed gratification" (see principle 1 of self-control), which is a predictor of later success.

Despite promising results, very little is being done in the schools themselves. The variety of training programs available is growing, but many schools are unwilling to introduce them. Of course, some investment is required. Moreover, many mental programs are as yet unable to present long-term results. Personally, I think we should seize the opportunity to carry out our own marshmallow experiment on a large scale. We would be making an investment that can yield a profit on several levels. The first results indicate that children who get the opportunity to strengthen their brains are less likely to be involved in crime later on, are physically and mentally healthier, are better at coping with stress and stronger in their professional and personal lives. In itself this seems to me like a very worthwhile investment indeed.

MAKING THE BRAIN ACCESSIBLE

By first creating awareness around the challenges of the current brain crisis as well as highlighting the possibilities that already exist, we create a climate in which investments are possible. Secondly, we must make the path to investment as accessible as possible. Since the 1990s, thousands have found the way to psychotherapy to find a solution for their psychological problems, but positive psychology still seems highly inaccessible to many people.

Here, too, I see a role in store for the government, which can remove a financial threshold by offering "mental resilience checks" which people can use to take certain courses and training programs to improve their mental and, by extension, physical health. The results of some mental training programs (such as mindfulness) are more convincing than those of certain drugs. The government could also offer concessions to businesses and organizations that introduce an Employee Assistance Program (EAP – a coaching and advice service for employees) around mental health, or implement an anti-burnout strategy throughout their entire company.

Stimulating better minds is crucial for business. Companies today have the opportunity to have a stress-risk analysis performed in order to find out how our minds can be strengthened. To do this, Better Minds at Work uses an online tool that probes the stress and engagement of employees. With this analysis we can assess where the painful areas lie within the company. We discovered at one major company that negative stress arose primarily around intergenerational conflicts. This result presented the opportunity to anticipate such problems and to make targeted adjustments before things have a chance to escalate.

In another company, the stress seemed to pile up due to numerous distractions, so that employees felt they were unable to work in a focused, goal-oriented way. In several departments, the situation has been addressed by introducing specific "elephant hours," in which employees can pursue their priorities without interruption.

When a company wants to develop a sustainable strategy around better minds and not stop at a one-time intervention – opting for an EAP is the logical next step. The introduction of an EAP for employees is often healing in itself. After all, it means that the company is showing concern for its employees and that the employees can get advice from an external advisory bureau. It is important to insist on customization, in which a program is fully adjusted to the needs of the particular company. Mental resilience is central to such an approach. Making employees aware that they can empower their brain. Offering training programs in which self-control, stress management, engagement and brain power are stimulated gives a business an extra advantage.

When we speak of an increase in mental strength, we also have to devote attention to our brain. We must optimize it and get the best out of it. In this sense, computer training that "stretches" the working memory can have a favorable effect on a person's attention span and self-control. This in turn can have a positive effect on the way he or she experiences stress. As noted earlier, a five-week training program is already sufficient to realize remarkable differences in the brain. More and more companies are seeing the added value of programs such as mindfulness training, for example, because it makes employees more aware of themselves and often has a positive effect on team spirit.

GROWING THROUGH CRISIS

Flu broke out in Mexico City in March 2009. Local health workers were immediately struck by the fact that this virus, in contrast to the usual annual flu, affected a striking number of young people. The alarm was sounded and, later, what a number of doctors already suspected was confirmed. It was a new kind of flu: variant N1H1 of the A virus.

Mexico resorted to stringent measures immediately. Schools, museums, libraries and other public buildings were closed, a state of emergency was declared, and Mexico City prepared to shut down the public transportation network. Meanwhile, however, the virus had spread to other countries. Less than a month later, the first cases turned up in the United States and Europe, where severe measures were also taken.

In the Netherlands, a toddler that had just returned from a family celebration in Mexico caused panic to break out. Everyone who had been near the child in the airplane was sought out and treated preventively. In several countries (from Lebanon to Azerbaijan), people were placed under quarantine. The Egyptian government ordered the immediate slaughter of all the pigs in the country. In June, the World Health Organization declared the outbreak of the virus a pandemic, effective immediately. The floodgates were open. The last time the word "pandemic" was used was when AIDS appeared in the 1980s, with more than 20 million deaths worldwide. The entire world was now under the sway of "swine flu" from Mexico.

At the end of 2009, the pandemic was measured for the first time. Worldwide, around 15,000 people had died of the virus. To compare: an average flu virus is responsible for 250,000 to 500,000 deaths per year.

This anticlimax led to a debate in many countries about the scare tactics orchestrated by the media and the government. Was it really necessary to create so much panic? But the World Health Organization answered in their defense that the pandemic couldn't have gone better. It was stopped before the virus had a chance to mutate. If the pandemic had shown anything, it was how resilient our healthcare system is and how strong our hospitals are in case of something as rare as a pandemic.

Our hospitals prepare for years in advance in order to be ready in case of disaster. They are trained to be "High Reliability Organizations" (HRO). HROs are organizations that in case of disaster have been proven to be reliable: from small fire departments that have succeeded in containing an extreme forest fire to companies that have survived a severe economic recession.

But you don't have to be a hospital or fire department to aspire to being an HRO – humans can do this too. There are many similarities between resilient organizations and resilient people. As people we will be confronted sooner or later with an unexpected event that will test our resilience.

However different the challenges faced by these organizations may be, according to research by Karl Weick at the University of Michigan, all HROs have a remarkable number of things in common in their response to a crisis.

First, they are not convinced of their own success – in fact, they're mentally prepared to fail. A second characteristic is related to the first: HROs call in the help of experts and trust more to the expertise of outsiders than their own assessments. Third, HROs examine each situation individually and seek solutions that suit the specific nature of the event. They also remain sensitive to the complexity of the situation and maintain an open mind at all times. The final characteristic that distinguishes HROs from other organizations is resilience.

The good news? We can all be an HRO if we want to, from individual to organization. It is mostly a matter of investing in the right things, the things we know will make us emerge triumphant from a crisis. I will try to be more specific with an example drawn from practice.

One day I got a call from a client, the CEO of a Dutch firm for which we had worked out a resilience program a year earlier. This time, Casper was calling with a personal question. He was very upset because he had just been invited for a talk with his bosses in Chicago. In all the years he'd worked for the company, this had never happened. What worried him was that a fellow CEO from Germany had received the same invitation a year earlier and was fired afterwards. Casper was expecting the worst.

STEP 1
INTERPRETATION

Like many people in this situation, Casper initially asked himself what he could have done to avoid this meeting. At the time, I pointed out that this was hardly a productive thought and that now, a month before the meeting, it would do him little good. The first step was to change his mindset about the upcoming talk.

Of course, I could have just comforted him by saying, "It will all come out well in the end," or, "Aren't you exaggerating a bit?" Instead, I suggested that he follow the strategy of an HRO and indeed assume a worst-case scenario. If the outcome was positive, there would be no limits to his happiness (we learned this earlier from research on the importance of surprise for experiencing happiness).

From other research we also know that it doesn't hurt to prepare for a negative situation, as long as you look at it from an optimistic perspective. If Casper were in fact to be fired, wasn't there a very good chance that, with his CV, he would quickly find a new and perhaps even better job? Gradually, Casper got used to the idea that this might be the end of his career with this company, but at the same time he began to worry about it less and less. Still, he decided that he would make the most of the meeting so that he could later look at it as a learning experience.

This kind of realistic optimism, as I suggested earlier, is quite specific to resilient people. They evaluate the situation no differently than pessimists, but they come up with a less negative interpretation of the facts. They literally see a silver lining in every cloud. It is not always easy to make the transition, but it is something we can encourage in ourselves. Self-control is the key to everything. Actively trying to control negative interpretations of facts in the present, or in the future to control and transform them, is the first step in the right direction.

You can compare the threat of Casper's impending meeting with the fear that rules the burnout and stress epidemic today. Too many executives still interpret this epidemic as something particularly negative, and of course that's important. It's also costing them a lot of money. What I also notice is that many executives get stuck on the blame question, which is ultimately unproductive. We can all choose to take responsibility by letting go of the annoyance and actively choosing to grow.

You can also interpret the challenges presented by stress and burnout positively, as a huge opportunity – not only for dealing with the crisis, but for using it as a chance to grow. A smart increase in mental capital gets you out of debt and has the potential to yield considerable profits. This crisis offers executives a unique chance to cash in on their mental capital.

STEP 2
IDENTIFICATION

Casper and I decided to assume the worst, but strive for the best. To this end, it was important to try to define the crisis very precisely. Under stress, people are inclined to assess situations unrealistically. The second step is also to become conscious of your unconscious thoughts about such an event. In Casper's mind, the meeting had escalated into into hours of agony and annoying questions, in which he would sit, sweating and stuttering, before a strict and unsympathetic jury.

This too may be familiar to many. Research confirms that if people have to evaluate a situation in the future, they almost always exaggerate. In a positive sense ("All my problems will be solved if I get this promotion"), but also in a negative sense ("If my partner leaves me, I'll never be happy again").

Instead of going along with his fantasies, we went after what we actually knew about the situation. We discovered that his estimation that he was about to be fired had little basis in fact. The message he had received was perhaps exceptional, but not at all as negative in tone as he had imagined. Then we looked into who would be present, where the conversation would take place, and how much time he would have. Here we applied the technique of visualization, so that he could imagine the situation in detail.

In this instance, Casper was pretty good at estimating what kind of crisis was coming at him. Of course, this is not always the case, but it happens more often than we might think. A trained athlete usually has a fairly good idea which muscles are susceptible to trauma during the practice of his or her specific discipline. In terms of mental health, most adults can also quickly identify their strengths and weaknesses, just as an executive knows the specific risks of his or her sector and a minister knows the weak spots of his or her terrain.

Identifying possible problems is something we all manage, although most people could use some help in this regard. An outsider often has better insight into the strengths and weaknesses of a person or organization. This is one of the reasons why a large social network contributes to personal resilience.

In the HRO model, this is called "appealing to resources for help." To increase their economic resilience, companies resort to an auditor, but their greatest risk zone (the mental resilience of their employees) all too often remains out of range. With Better Minds at Work, we see during the screening of a company exactly which department or what teams are susceptible to stress and burnout. This kind of preparation is not foolproof, but it increases the response time considerably in the event problems do arise.

STEP 3
CREATING AN OPEN MIND

Once we had the situation clear in our minds, we could write scenarios together, each time setting out a mind map. What questions would they ask? What criticisms would they offer? What if someone made this suggestion or had that reaction? Even the most unlikely situations were reviewed until Casper was prepared for everything – literally everything.

The point of this exercise was not so much to be exhaustive as to open the mind to new possibilities. We are naturally highly inclined to see only our side of the story and therefore to apply the same solutions every time. Part of resilience is learning to put yourself in someone else's shoes and follow a different reasoning than your own.

Not only did Casper acquire a more open mind this way, his confidence also got a boost. If he could come up with an appropriate response to all these scenarios, then he could probably do so in another. Moreover, I taught him how he could take the lead in each scenario and in this way turn the meeting to his advantage. By always coming back to thinking up solutions to new scenarios in all of our sessions, we reached a point at which this became routine for him. And routine, as we have seen, allows for flow.

We cannot predict the unpredictable, but we can learn to deal with the unexpected. By seeking out new challenges, we not only learn more about the challenges themselves, we also become expert in dealing with challenges. That's one of the reasons why travel is so enriching. After a distant journey, you may have already forgotten everything you saw after a few months, but the experience of having to cope with unknown situations and strange people lasts a lifetime.

This principle is also familiar in the business world. Resilient companies are companies that allow their employees to step out of their comfort zone and seek out new experiences, even if they have nothing to do with their work. The best-known example is Google, which has for years offered a "20 percent program," in which employees can invest one fifth of their time in projects that are unrelated to their actual job.

By making out-of-the-box thinking routine, you increase not only resilience, but also creativity and productivity. New challenges and the feeling of freedom are important conditions for employee engagement.

STEP 4
MENTAL PREPARATION

While we went over the various scenarios, we not only talked about the content, but also devoted considerable discussion to what was going on in his head. With such a challenge, in which the prospect of a reward is doubtful, it is only normal that Casper had to find resistance within himself at a given moment. During difficult times, we used distraction to maintain his self-control. I also kept an eye on his reserves to make sure he didn't use up his supply before the big day. It's better to do a little each day than a lot in a short time. As we have seen, when preserving self-control, it's important not to hand out too many rewards along the way (such as compliments). In this way, we kept our focus constantly trained on the final goal.

Casper also had trouble with straying thoughts on a regular basis. I therefore suggested that, in the month before his conversation, he pay more attention than ever to his physical condition: eating healthy food, exercising once a week or taking walks, and above all getting enough sleep. In the run-up to an important event, most people do the opposite. They start eating unhealthily, skimping on exercise, forgetting to take time out for themselves and sleeping less. From the point of view of your brain, this is probably the worst possible strategy. Anyone who wants to meet a challenge with the right mind not only needs to train, but also to respect the basic rules of mental hygiene.

In this case, it wasn't necessary to work on increasing focus because Casper was already highly focused on his goal. Instead, we paid particular attention to developing an optimistic attitude, maintaining motivation through self-control, and training his consciousness. It goes without saying that all of these things would be useful above and beyond the upcoming meeting.

Of all the steps you can take in a crisis, increasing mental resilience in the long term is certainly the most important. In this part of the preparation lies the key to post-traumatic growth, which determines whether what doesn't kill us does indeed make us stronger. Of course most people take steps to acquire mental training only when a crisis arrives. But that's not necessarily a disadvantage. An acute threat could result in people demonstrating even more perseverance in training. And a second advantage is that in a crisis they will quickly see the results of their investment, so that they keep investing afterwards.

For Casper this was indeed the case. Because he was so well prepared, the meeting in Chicago went much better than expected. Even though doubts were indeed expressed at the beginning of the discussion, the atmosphere at the end was very positive and it turned out to be a win-win situation for both parties. A couple of bosses who had never met him personally were so impressed that they have since begun to consult him on major decisions. In this way, he was able to turn a negative situation into a positive turning point in his career.

Casper was not weakened by this crisis – it made him stronger. He is now more effective, stronger and more focused than ever. Casper has become an HRO. And this is something we can all do. By throwing our brain into the fray, we can survive the current brain crisis and even grow because of it. Let's seize the day and start working on a better mind for us all.

Relevant literature

. . . .

PART I: A WAY THROUGH
THE BRAIN CRISIS

Portrait of a burnout

Kelly McGonigal (2015). *The upside of stress: Why stress is good for you and how to get good at it.* New York: Avery/Penguin.

Resilience, or the law of the stimulative arrears

Jan Romein (1935). "De dialectiek van de vooruitgang." *Forum,* 4.
Steven Joseph (2011). *What doesn't kill us: The new psychology of posttraumatic growth.* New York: Basic Books.
Arnold Bakker & Michael Leiter (2011). *Work engagement: A handbook of essential theory and research.* New York: Psychology Press.
Mihalyi Csikszentmihalyi (1990). *Flow: The psychology of optimal experience.* New York: Harper and Row.
Abraham Maslow (1943). "A theory of human motivation." *Psychological Review,* 50, pp. 370-396.

PART II: PROFITING
FROM RESILIENCE

Don't think about the marsh-
mallow: The value of self control

A.L. Duckworth, C. Peterson, M.D. Matthews & D. Kelly (2007). "Grit: Perseverance and passion for long-term goals." *Journal of Personality and Social Psychology,* 92, pp. 1087-1101.
W. Mischel, Y. Shoda, & M.L. Rodriguez (1989). "Delay of gratification in children." *Science,* 244, pp. 933-938.
Amy Chua (2011). *Battle Hymn of the Tiger Mother.* New York: Penguin Books.
Daniel Wegner (1989). *White bears and other unwanted thoughts: Suppression, obsession, and the psychology of mental control.* New York: Viking/Penguin.
Roy Baumeister & John Tierney (2011). *Willpower: Rediscovering the greatest human strength.* New York: Penguin Books.

Why Archimedes ran naked through the streets: Consciously engaging your consciousness

Bernard Baars (1988). *A cognitive theory of consciousness*. New York: Cambridge University Press.

M.A. Killingsworth & D.T. Gilbert (2010). "A wandering mind is an unhappy mind." *Science*, 330, p. 932.

W. Hasenkamp, C.D. Wilson-Mendenhall, E. Duncan & L.W. Barsalou (2012). "Mind wandering and attention during focused meditation: a fine-grained temporal analysis of fluctuating cognitive states." *Neuroimage*, 59, pp. 750-760.

Perla Kaliman, María Jesús Álvarez-López, Marta Cosín-Tomás, Melissa A. Rosenkranz, Antoine Lutz, & Richard J. Davidson (2014). "Rapid changes in histone deacetylases and inflammatory gene expression in expert meditators." *Psychoneuroendocrinology*, 40, pp. 96-107.

How you really play "I'm going on a trip and I'm taking ... ": The importance of focus

Thomas H. Davenport & John C. Goldhaber (2001). *The attention economy: Understanding the new currency of business*. Boston: Harvard Business Review Press.

Daniel Goleman (2013). *Focus: The hidden driver of excellence*. New York: Harper Collins.

George A. Miller (1956). "The magical number seven, plus or minus two: Some limits on our capacity for processing information." *Psychological Review*, 63, pp. 81-97.

Torkel Klingberg, Hans Forssberg & Helena Westerberg (2002). "Training of Working Memory in Children with ADHD." *Journal of Clinical and Experimental Neuropsychology*, 24, pp. 781-791.

Fiona McNab, Andrea Varrone, Lars Farde, Aurelija Jucaite, Paulina Bystritsky, Hans Forssberg & Torkel Klingberg (2009). "Changes in cortical dopamine D1 receptor binding associated with cognitive training." *Science*, 323, pp. 800-802.

The explanation for everything: The power of optimism

Barbara Ehrenreich (2010). *Smile or die: How positive thinking fooled America and the world*. London: Granta.

Martin Seligman (2011). *Flourish: A visionary new understanding of happiness and well-being*. New York: Atria Books.

Barbara Fredrickson (2009). *Positivity: Top-notch research reveals the upward spiral that will change your life*. New York: Crown.

**PART III: FOUR WAYS TO ARRIVE
AT A BETTER BRAIN STRATEGY**

*The 47-percent rule: Investing
in present and absent time*
Andrew P. Knight & Markus Baer
(2014). "Get up, stand up. The effects
of a non-sedentary workspace on
information elaboration and group
performance." *Social Psychological
and Personality Science*, 5, pp. 910-917.
Arianna Huffington (2014). *Thrive:
The third metric to redefining success
and creating a life of well-being,
wisdom, and wonder.* New York:
Harmony Books.

*Divide space and conquer:
Choose focus in an
infinite space*
Theo Compernolle (2014). *Brain
Chains.* Tielt: Lannoo.
Tom DeMarco & Timothy Lister
(1987). *Peopleware: Productive Projects
and Teams.* New York: Dorset House.
Sandra Bond Chapman & Shelly
Kirkland (2014). *Make your brain
smarter: Increase your brain's creativity,
energy, and focus.* New York: Simon
and Schuster.
Eyal Ophir, Clifford Nass, & Anthony
Wagner (2009). "Cognitive control in
media multitaskers." *Proceedings of
the National Academy of Sciences*, 106,
pp. 15583-15587.

Kep Kee Loh and Ryota Kanai
(2014). "High media multi-tasking is
associated with smaller gray-matter
density in the anterior cingulate
cortex." *PLOS ONE*, 9, pp. 1-7.

*It's not at all lonely at the top:
Motivation in connection*
Brené Brown (2011). *Daring Greatly:
How the courage to be vulnerable
transforms the way we live, love, parent,
and lead.* New York: Gotham/Penguin
Group.
Teresa Amabile & Steven Kramer
(2011). *The Progress Principle: Using
Small Wins to Ignite Joy, Engagement,
and Creativity at Work.* Boston:
Harvard Business Review Press.
Daniel H. Pink (2009). *Drive: The surprising truth about what motivates us.*
New York: Riverhead/Penguin Group.

*Our optimal brain:
A strategy for better minds*
James J. Heckman (2013). *Giving
kids a fair chance.* Cambridge,
Massachusetts: Boston Review
Groups/MIT Press.
Paul Tough (2013). *How children
succeed: Grit, curiosity, and the hidden
power of character.* Boston: Houghton
Mifflin Harcourt.
Jelle Jolles (2011). *Ellis en het
verbreinen.* Amsterdam: Neuropsych
Publishers.

Maarten Vansteenkiste & Bart
Soenens (2013). *Vitamines van groei –
Over de motiverende rol van ouders in
de opvoeding.* Ghent: Academia Press.
Lisa Flook, Simon B.Goldberg, Laura
Pinger & Richard J.Davidson (2015).
"Promoting prosocial behavior and
self-regulatory skills in preschool
children through a mindfulness-
based kindness curriculum."
Developmental Psychology, 51, pp. 44-51.

**CONCLUSION: GROWING
THROUGH CRISIS**

Karl E. Weick & Kathleen M. Sutcliffe
(2007). *Managing the unexpected:
Resilient performance in an age of
uncertainty.* Hoboken: John Wiley &
Sons.205

Index

www.lannoo.com

www.elkegeraerts.com

Translation Irene Schaudies

Cover design Studio Jan de Boer

Author photo Liesbet Peremans

© Uitgeverij Lannoo nv and Elke Geraerts, 2017

D/2017/45/675 – ISBN 978 94 014 4894 9 – NUR 770